For Love of the Miniature Horse

A Collection of Heartwarming Miniature Horse Stories & Poems

Compiled and Edited by
Kathy Atchley

⌡] RonJon Publishing, Inc.

Editor and Compiler
Kathy Atchley

Design Layout, Illustrations, Cover Design
Nicholas Inglish

© 2001   RonJon Publishing, Inc.

ISBN 1-56870-428-3

First Edition

Printed in the United States of America

For information, contact:
RonJon Publishing, Inc.
1001 S. Mayhill Rd.
Denton, Texas 76208
(940) 383-3060
Information@ronjonpublishing.com

My two favorite things are miniature horses and book editing, so I have combined them both in this labor of love. I hope you enjoy reading the stories as much as I have enjoyed compiling them for you.

Kathy Atchley

All stories are published with the permission
of the authors.

Original painting on cover courtesy of
Jody Chenoweth

Table of Contents

Miniature Horses: A Collection of Short Stories

Life With A Miniature Horse

You whinnied shrilly to your playmates as I led you away
Seeming so tiny and helpless when I bought you that day
I taught you to come when called and to lead
You learned so quickly as I saw to your needs
Soon becoming a beloved member of our family
With your character and style it was quite easy
Always the center of attention wherever we go
The darling of schools, nursing homes, parades, and shows
You stand steadily to be stroked by Grandma's trembling, loving hand
But prance and dance in the parades to the sound of the band
You were patiently there through it all
When my spirit soared high or plummeted in a fall
When the time came for my Grandmother to die
You shared in my grief as in your stall I cried
Alone, your mane soaked with tears, I said my good-bye
She had finally shed her frail body, now her spirit could fly!
I'm uncertain of just when the roles were reversed
When the caretaker became the taken care of, I'm just not sure
A friend is someone to cherish with a heart of pure gold
A friend listens patiently and keeps your secrets untold
I have found respite in the sweet pungent smell of your hide
I've known solace when I look into your all-knowing eyes
You were there whickering softly each time I came near
Always ready to hear my joy, sorrow, or fears
If I had it to do all over again I'd choose the same course
And share my life, love, and family with a Miniature Horse!

By Linda Rodriguez
Havenbrook Miniature Horse Farm
Burkesville, Kentucky
http://www.angelfire.com/biz4/havenbrook/

The Story of Striker and Ira

By Sue High
Flying High Farm
Flower Mound, Texas
http://members.home.net/flyinghighfarm

This story is for horse lovers who think that big horses and minis cannot coexist. There are so many stories that I could tell of their adventures over the past couple of years, but the most amazing one is how our little horse with the big heart saved his big buddy.

My husband and I moved to a small farm in the summer of 1997. I missed my horses, which I had given up for family reasons a few years earlier. Within a month, we had adopted a 16-hand, retired hunter/jumper named "I Dare Ya," or Ira for short. To keep him company, we boarded an aged mare, named Sadie, for a friend of mine.

In the fall of 1999, the mare's cancer advanced to the stage where she had to be put to sleep. Ira was so lonely and frantic that we had to find him a companion quickly. We didn't want to buy another big horse because I am unable to ride any longer due to old injuries in my back and neck. One of my friends suggested that we get a miniature horse. We talked about it, decided it might be a good solution to our problem, and I started doing some research. My main concern was that they would not get along. Ira is very mellow, but he is still very large and an accidental kick or bite would be devastating to a small horse. My husband was headed out of town on a business trip and I remember his parting words, "When you find a mini that you want, don't put it in the back of my Suburban to bring it home and don't drain the bank account!"

I called several folks who had placed ads in the local newspaper and I searched the Internet ads. I wanted a gelding. He had to be very friendly and easy-going. It didn't take me long to find just what I was looking for. Actually, he was even more than I had hoped for! I spoke to Kathy Atchley of Sunrise Hill Farm. I told her about my dilemma and she said she had a possible fit for me. I spent a couple of hours that afternoon looking at several of her minis and getting an education. The horse that I went to see was a nice little guy, but I fell in love with a driving gelding that Kathy had for sale.

He was a 2-1/2-year-old son of Lucky Four Strike Me Silver named Lucky Four Silvers Striking (Striker for short). Being a total novice, the pedigree meant nothing to me. All I cared about was that he was extremely outgoing. I had never driven a horse, so his trainer, Wendy O'Neill, gave me a quick lesson in the round pen. My neighbor had come with me to shoot video so that I could show all of the horses to my husband when he returned from his trip. All you see in this video is me going around the big round pen with Striker, and I was giggling the whole time! It was so much fun!

Needless to say, I just had to have Striker, and Kathy delivered him to our farm the next day (I explained to her about the Suburban thing and she understood!). We brought Striker to the fence. Ira took one look at him and bolted in the other direction! Then Ira came back, sniffed Striker through the fence, and decided that since he smelled like a horse and looked like a horse, albeit an awfully little one, he must be a horse. We turned them out together and they have been best friends ever since! Striker was not the least bit intimidated by Ira.

Ira and Striker are like Mutt and Jeff. They get along marvelously. Since Striker is so much younger than Ira, I think he keeps him young. He loves to play and the two of them are a blast to watch. Striker can literally walk under Ira. Ira herds him around. Striker steals the hay. Mutual-grooming is a little tricky, but they have worked it out. I have since bought a couple of mares, but we keep them in a separate pasture. They are afraid of Ira. Striker isn't afraid of anything!

Just before Christmas this past year, I went out to feed at the usual time in the morning, but Ira wouldn't come into his stall to eat. He just stood outside looking at me. He is 26 years old and he occasionally decides to skip a meal, so I wasn't terribly alarmed. I decided I would finish feeding everyone else, take my son to school, and then see if I could get him to eat. I looked him over and found no evidence of rolling. I found fresh manure too, so I thought he was in no imminent danger.

When I returned 20 minutes later, I became alarmed. As I pulled in, I saw Ira trying to lie down and Striker rushing in and attacking him! I ran to the pasture. My husband saw me through the window and came running too, not knowing what had happened. As I ran to the barn for Ira's halter, Striker

Striker and Ira.

repeated his attacks on Ira. If you didn't know the two horses, you would have thought that this miniature horse was horribly mean. He pawed at Ira's neck and bit his flanks each time that Ira hit the ground, and he wouldn't let up until Ira got up. How Striker knew that he had to keep Ira from rolling is anybody's guess. As we all know, if Ira had been allowed to roll during his colic attack, he could have twisted his intestines, which is often fatal. My husband witnessed the whole thing, otherwise, I feared no one would believe me!

I got the halter on Ira and started to lead him around. My husband ran for the phone. The vet arrived within ten minutes. I told her what had happened. She was incredulous! She had never seen or heard of such a thing. Striker stayed glued to Ira's side as I walked Ira while waiting for the vet and the entire time the vet was there to treat Ira. He sniffed every instrument she used and made a general nuisance of himself, but we let him stay.

Since Striker seemed to have such an uncanny sense of when Ira was sick, we let them stay together as Ira recovered. Once more that day and again two weeks later, Striker alerted me to the fact that Ira wasn't doing well by his attacks on Ira. I have pictures of the two of them lying side-by-side sleeping, so I know that he doesn't always attack Ira when he lies down. It is amazing how Striker just seems to know when his big buddy is hurting!

The vet feels that Ira must have begun his colic attack before I went out to feed that morning and the reason I saw no evidence that Ira had rolled was due to Striker's vigil through the night. Ira was suffering from liver problems that manifested themselves in colic. He is on medication now and has suffered no more attacks, from colic *or* Striker, since January.

I am not saying that all big horses and all miniature horses can have this kind of a friendship. You must always factor in the personalities of each animal before you try to put them together. We know that we are enormously blessed to have Striker! He is a remarkable little horse. He loves people of all ages (especially children) and other animals. He is "Uncle Striker" to my miniature foals and he will be Ira's best friend until the day he dies.

But What Are They Good For?

By Sharon K. Taylor
Mystic Rose Ranch
Jackson, California
www.horseminiature.net

For 92-year-old Bea Miller, every day was pretty much the same. The aides at the nursing home would wake her each morning, dress her, and take her into a larger lounge area where she would spend her day. Since she required a greater level of care, she had been transferred from another facility a few weeks before, and the staff had never met nor been contacted by any family members. Her bill was paid through a trust account. Though the aides tried to find some activity that she would enjoy, they were always met with a blank stare and little or no emotion. It was clear to most that Bea's days were quickly coming to an end. But Bea's life changed one August morning.

Each month Mystic Rose Ranch takes two or three miniature horses to community events, local parades, elementary schools, or, in this case, to visit the local convalescent home. Residents who were able to leave their rooms waited for us in an outside patio. As we walked the horses up to each resident, photos were taken so they might have a visual memory of the day and something to later show family and friends.

The staff may have felt they were simply going through the motions when they approached Bea with four-month-old Mystic Rose Small Fortune. But rather than being met with the same blank stare they were accustomed to, Bea surprised them. It took a moment for her to realize what was nuzzling her hand, but when she did, something clicked. Bea's eyes came to life, she reached out to Small Fortune—and she appeared to smile. There was later speculation that Bea might have once owned her own horse and that this visit had triggered a memory that may have been buried for decades. The next day we delivered the photos to the nursing home, and when Bea's photo was presented to her, we were told she reached out and clutched it. It remained in her hand the rest of the day and became the first item she reached for each morning. Over the next two weeks, the crumpled photo was replaced several times until the staff finally had one laminated for her.

Sadly, Bea died that September. We received a call from the nurses whom we had come to know well. The unit manager told us no family had claimed Bea's body, so the social worker made the proper arrangements with the funeral home. The casket was modest. There would be no funeral. But she did make a

**Bea Miller with
Mystic Rose Small Fortune.**

request of the funeral director. "Please bury Bea in her favorite blue sweater. And, oh yes, would it be possible to place Small Fortune's photo in her hands?"

Like most owners of miniature horses, we are asked from time to time, "But what good are they if you can't ride them?" How can we begin to describe what one small horse meant to a dying woman who had given up on life?

Faith

By John Tuttle, DVM
Tuttle Veterinary Clinic
Basehor, Kansas

Foaling season, as many of you may already know, can have its ups and downs. It can be very satisfying emotionally as well as financially, but at times it can be an agonizing "season" as well. Foaling problems, or *dystocias*, can occur with any breed of horse, but are more common in the miniature horse due of course to their size and conformation. I am sure everyone has their "stories"—thought I'd share a humbling one which occurred to me.

Early Easter Sunday, I received a call from Theresa Gergick of Promise Me Miniatures. One of her mares was having problems foaling. After arriving I examined the situation and found the mare to have the foal partially presented with only the head and part of one front leg being presented. This type of dystocia, especially in miniatures, proves to be one of the more disturbing, being as the head begins swelling rather rapidly due to restriction of blood flow from the head. This can make it rather difficult to reposition the foal to retrieve the other front leg, as the foal normally has to be pushed back in to achieve this. In the smaller miniatures it does not leave much time or room to work.

Unfortunately, in the majority of cases, the foal is already dead, necessitating amputation of the head to repel the foal back in to reposition the leg(s). Upon examining the foal, there were no signs of life— no eye response, no sucking response, the tongue was hanging out of the mouth, the eyelids were beginning to swell—all in all, a pretty bleak outlook for the foal. The thought of telling Theresa and her family of the probable procedure I was most likely going to have to do to this foal, was to say the least, upsetting.

All of Theresa's nieces and nephews were there for Easter Sunday and had made a small circle around the mare, Theresa and me. They were watching silently, their eyes big with wonderment and concern. As I took a deep breath, preparing myself for what I was going to tell them, I heard the weakest, most faint little nicker you can ever imagine! I immediately shifted my attention back to the foal—no change in appearance—it must have been wishful "hearing." As I leaned even closer to re-evaluate the situation, I'll be darned if I didn't hear something that sounded like a whispering nicker. Much to my amazement and disbelief, the foal was still alive!

Cedar Hill Power of Faith.

After rushing back to the truck for additional OB lube (Theresa must have thought I'd been stung on the butt by a bee), the mare was sedated and given a spinal, and I was hoping to get this foal repositioned without losing it or the mare. During the procedure, the mare had laid down, making it necessary for me to lie down with her. After what seemed like hours, which was most likely minutes, we got the foal repositioned and were able to begin assisting the mare with delivery. Still not knowing if the foal was going to make it through all of this stress, we assisted the mare in the presentation through the birth canal.

As we readied ourselves for the final "pull," the mare had a strong contraction, the foal was delivered rather abruptly (which, by that time, ended up nearly on my chest), and within seconds of being born, raised its head up and gave a nicker which would choke up any horseperson. It was like a nicker which said, "Wow! Thanks, that was close!"

The foal was a filly and was promptly named Faith. Theresa was in tears, but I think I was the only one who noticed—and for some reason, she didn't mind me putting my dirty arm around her. My hat goes off to Theresa, because if she had not been on top of the situation, things would not have turned out as well…and I would not have this fond Easter memory to share with you. Funny…it still puts that lump in my throat after all this time.

Mundy's Miracle

By Nancy Goshorn
Galloping G Minis
Reedsville, Pennsylvania
http://minibreeders.com/gallopinggminis

Mustardseed Ramundos Summer Dream 8/29/88 – 8/27/00

In February of 2000, I went to feed our minis. It was around 4 p.m. I noticed Mundy was just picking at her feed. I called the vet and he arrived later that evening. A blood test was done, but he wasn't overly concerned. He said to start giving her Karo syrup every hour, till he got back to me in the a.m., which I did. Late that evening was when I turned to the miniature horse forum. I was in a panic till morning, as someone suggested it might be hyperlipemia. Confirmation came in the morning, but the vet thought she would be fine with the Karo and some extra attention (he didn't have her triglyceride level) and to be sure she was eating. Back to the forum, where I was told, don't wait, get on it now, she could be dead in three days. I felt so helpless and cried many tears for her. Not my Mundy, she had to live. I called the vet and wanted IVs started. They were not set up for that, so I called an equine vet over the mountain and immediately took Mundy to their hospital.

She was started on IV and several meds. He did a blood test but said it would be two days before he got the results. My daughter, Holly, works for Dr. Braunstine and they have the means for a complete read-out of bloodwork. He agreed to allow her to go to the clinic at midnight to run the complete blood test. It didn't look good. Her triglyceride level was 3900. Back to the forum, where I was told there is little hope, if these levels are over 1200. It was suggested that I put her down. I couldn't give up on Mundy. She and I had a special, almost magical bond between us. Dr. McCalister didn't hold out much hope for Mundy, but was willing to do all he could for her. She became very weak and could hardly stand. She was at the hospital for almost five weeks. Her muscles were so weak from standing in one spot for so

Nancy with Mundy on the road to recovery.

long. When she tried to lie down, she dislocated her hip! Many days while there, the vet thought she wouldn't make it through the night. He would say, I don't know what is keeping her alive. I told him, it was a miracle, from above.

She was sent home with me when she started eating small amounts of alfalfa. Dr. McCalister said we had to get her stronger before we even thought about her hip. I hand-fed her almost every bite of food that she took. Apples, carrots, special feeds, just to have her take a nibble or two. Mundy was in foal and I was told there was next to zero hope of a live foal and that I should just be thankful that Mundy was still hanging on. I was thankful and very happy. Mundy is a sweet, precious mare with a strong will to live. She melted my heart each time she looked at me with her big, soft, puppy-dog eyes.

Mundy had a terrible discharge starting March 6th. She wasn't due until April 18th. The vet came back again and thought she was about to abort the foal. He said if it was alive when it was born, it would most likely die, or not live long. It was going to be premature and also from all the medicines and the fact that Mundy was still very weak.

Two weeks later, I knew by the look in Mundy's eye that day of March 20th, that this was the day. I alerted the vet, he said he would stop by sometime the next day to check her. He hoped I wouldn't be too upset at the loss of the foal. I said maybe, just maybe it will be a fighter like its mama. Galloping G Evidence Of A Miracle arrived at 9:40 p.m. Very tiny, 7 lbs., 8 oz. and very weak. Her little legs went every which way. After an hour or so of trying to help her stand to eat,

I got out the baby bottle. My next two days were spent in the barn, in the hay, snuggled up with Mundy and Evie. That is such a warm, beautiful memory. I spent many hours rocking and singing to Evie. She seemed to love it as much as I did. Evie soon got the hang of nursing (ahhhh, I get to sleep) and I continued to rock her until she was weaned at 3-1/2 months. The vet wanted to do surgery on Mundy's leg. It had locked up tight from the weakness and lack of muscle tone.

The week of surgery, when Mundy was trying to lie down, she flopped down so hard, she dislocated her other hip. Dr. McCalister called New Bolten Center. They said surgery was just about out of the question as there is no way to manage her after surgery. Suggested was, again, put her down, or let her stand in a stall/small area and hope that the bones would fuse. Dr. McCalister and Dr. Ed agreed to give her to the end of July and we could then make a decision.

Through all this, Mundy was a sweetheart and after the first week, seemed to have no pain. I didn't want to put her down, but would have done so if she was suffering. At the beginning of August, she started getting around really well. She loved all the attention she was given and our bond grew stronger and stronger. I have never loved a horse, or any animal, the way I loved Mundy. She brought a smile to my face each morning, as she gave her soft nicker, to greet me. She was spoiled, loved and pampered each day. She was getting all of my attention. I had decided it was time to stop rocking Evie. She needed to learn to get along with the other foals. She was not happy, and walked around with her head down, pouting, for almost a week. Broke my heart, that little one.

On August 22nd I called Dr. McCalister and said Mundy is really improving. I think it's time for her surgery. I could hardly wait. I knew she would be able to get around even better. I was so happy for her, after all the trials, she was going to make it. He was going to come check her the following week.

Sunday evening, August 27th, around 11 p.m., our German shepherd started barking. He was barking like I had never heard before. I got the flashlight to go see what was going on. It kept going out on me, so I went back in the house. I then went back outside to jump on the golf cart and drive around back. For some unknown reason, I jumped in the car instead. (Thank God.) I had never done this before, to go just around the back of the house. When I got there, I saw Mundy, but couldn't quite decide what I was seeing. I thought there was a black tarp or something around her. I opened the car door, with the lights still shining on her and then, I realized it was a huge black bear! He had gotten into the fence and was pulling and biting Mundy, trying to drag her back over the fence. I screamed, I blew the car horn, I pounded the side of the car. The bear stood up (at least six feet tall) and looked at me and then grabbed my Mundy again.

I raced to the house screaming. My husband had just gotten up from bed to see what was going on. I screamed, please help Mundy, hurry, he is killing her, please hurry, get your gun. Hurry, hurry, please help her. I felt so helpless. He grabbed the gun and the flashlight that wasn't working right. When he got to the back yard, the light went out. He fired the gun to scare the bear away. He couldn't see him. He got another light, and I drove back around to help Mundy, saying please, please Mundy, don't be dead. It was too late, she was gone. I was screaming, no, no, no, not Mundy. It was horrible, terrifying, heartbreaking. I was in shock and kept repeating, Oh Mundy, I'm sorry, I'm so sorry, Mundy. You didn't deserve to die like this after all you've been through.

We called the state police and the game commissioners. About an hour later, as we were waiting for them to show up, my husband, son, and son-in-law were out back with Mundy. While standing there this big bear (400 lbs.) came charging up the bank. He was claiming his kill. My husband fired a shot and he ran. We knew he was hit from all the blood. When the police and commissioners arrived, they started the search. While looking, they found six or seven places in our other fences that he had tried to get in. In fact, we believe he was in the one larger field (the fence was torn clear down). I guess he couldn't catch one so easily. Bears don't want to expend too much energy for a kill as they are trying to put on as much fat as possible for winter. That field was just a short distance from Mundy. Mundy was in a smaller area, with a shorter, panel-type fence. Around 3 a.m., they found the bear, down near the horses in the lower field. When he turned toward them, he was shot and killed.

This was not a normal bear. He had been killing sheep, goats and more in our area. He came through corn fields and passed by pear and apple trees to get to my horses. The evening before, my grandchildren were playing, near dark, in the same area. I can't help but think that

Mundy may have saved a child's life that night. Rest in peace, my precious one. I will always remember this very special mare, and the wonderful times we shared together. I thank God for the wonderful little miracle she left behind. I love you, Mundy!

Postscript #1: My granddaughter, Tiffany, came to our door yesterday, early in the morning. She had Evie and said, "Gram, she's sad, rock her." She brought her in the house, and put her over my lap (my, has she grown). As I was rocking her, I started singing and bless her heart, she went limp, eyes closed, head hanging. Just like old times, she was out like a light. Mundy will live on in this precious miracle she left behind!

Postscript #2: Evie was taken to her first show in the summer of 2001 and took a first and second in her yearling halter class!

Cody, The Dancing Mini

By Dianne Rossi
The Magical World of Dancing Horses
Pico Rivera, California
www.worldofdancinghorses.com

My best friends and I bought Cody, a black dwarf miniature horse, at four months old. None of us had ever had a miniature before and we fell in love with the little guy, promising the breeder we would take very good care of him. I have a show of dancing horses and I wanted to use him in my show and he was such a good-looking little guy, he captured our hearts. I had no idea how much these little fellows liked people since I have only handled the big guys my whole career.

By the time we got Cody home, I swear he looked like a miniature buffalo. I never saw so much hair. We cooed and ogled over him, telling him was the prettiest boy in the world. To an onlooker who was non-involved, I'm sure they thought us certifiable, hugging and kissing this ball of fur that certainly didn't look very pretty at all.

He could run very, very fast, seeming to lose three inches in height and then stop on a dime and prance and strut, which was pretty hard with legs his size. He has a red manure tub that he can roll at full speed without missing a beat, then go down on his knees and go inside attacking the "tub man." So much personality in a little package. I could hide carrots behind my back and he would walk around and get them. So unlike a large horse. He was our pride and joy.

I had to go to a convention for my show and decided to take Cody for publicity, less his buffalo appearance. What a surprise when we found that we really did have a very cute compact guy, even smaller than we thought, losing two inches after the clip job. He was the hit of the convention and he never tired of people wanting to pet and scratch him.

Disaster hit at eight months and we loaded him into the van and off to a specialist. We found he was allergic to almost everything causing a reaction and that was affecting his breathing. Seems like everything in the breathing department is stuffed into small areas in these little horses. After ten days of intensive care we were given back our boy with pills and medication and not too much hope. We put his pen up in the spa area and completely shut off his world with plastic and he became our Bubble Baby. We doctored him day and night and his house was by the bedroom window so we could hear every move he made. We even had an asthma sprayer that had to be used in his nose three times a day. It was like taking care of a human baby.

It's Show Time!

He started getting better and we could then lead him around the yard to stretch his legs, but no exertion was allowed until we could get him on an allergy medication and have time for it to take hold. How do you tell a kid that he can't run and play when he's starting to feel good? We prevailed and after a week of shots he could contain himself no longer and he began using his little pen for a race track. It was one of the happiest days of our lives.

The recovery was mostly good, but he did go up and down for almost a year. He will be on allergy injections the rest of his life. End of story? No way! Cody is now four years old, a big 22" tall, and all boy. He's very pushy and very naughty, but he's our naughty and we love him every bit for it. We left him a stallion by preference, to retain his personality and buff appearance. Our big Friesian mare is "his woman," and she thinks he's pretty neat, too.

He has become the star of the show along with his 26" buddy, "Little Willie Tickle Britches." Billed as the "Magic Ponies," both minis run out into the arena and mount their pedestals. Carefully edited music and voice-overs make both ponies appear to talk and sing as they shake their heads up and down to the music of Alvin and the Chipmunks. The audience is in tears of laughter by the time the act is over. In another segment we call "Shrink the Friesian," a 17-hand

Friesian is put into a shrinking machine and through a series of fun props and plays, out runs Cody very, very fast. He seems to love it. Cody bows, rears and turns very fast tight twirls. He can do other tricks too, but I have to grovel on the ground to get them…so we leave those out of the act!

Coming soon to The Magical World of Dancing Horses is Tiny Tail. This palomino colt stands 17" tall and we expect him to be the same size as Cody. He will join Cody in the act.

Angel's First Show

By Nancy Brehm
Mini Happy Returns Miniatures
Abilene, Texas
nancy_brehm@yahoo.com

The morning was clear and beautiful as my husband, Mike, and I reviewed all the last-minute details of taking our five little horses to the AMHA show at the West Texas Fair and Rodeo in Abilene, Texas. This would be the first show experience for three of the horses since they were this year's spring babies. There was Rambo, who since birth seemed to exude self-confidence and a great attitude; Choco, who was sweet and a little shy; and finally there was Angel, our beautiful black and white filly with a blue eye who, despite her diminutive size (25.25"), was afraid of nothing to the point of being almost too passive.

Starting in her first class, it was clear that Angel was not too interested in competing. She was cooperative but lacked that sparkle that we all look for in our miniature show horses. However, she remained curious about her surroundings and all the spectators that came by her stall. The horses were housed in the sheep and goat barn, so their stalls were made of chain-link fencing making easy access for any fair-goers who wanted to pet the horses.

The day of the show was also the day the fair had specified as free entry for anyone mentally or physically disabled, so a number of those passing through the barn fell into this category. One such person was a little boy named Brad who was about eight years old and suffered with cerebral palsy. I was standing in a crowded area waiting to take Angel into her color class when Brad and his mother wheeled near me and were momentarily stopped by the crowds. His little arms and legs were uncontrollably moving about and his facial expressions were quite contorted. I discovered from his mother that Brad also was nearly blind but did have peripheral vision. I asked if I could take his hand and let him pet Angel. She had already taken the initiative to nuzzle this little boy, but then as I took Brad's hand, I told him that Angel loved little boys. I then moved his hand over so it gently stroked her soft hair. Almost immediately, Brad's legs and arms seemed to relax and cease moving and his face lit up with a huge grin. He made a kind of moaning sound that his mother interpreted as one of great pleasure. She remarked that he is normally so frightened of new people or animals and that she was amazed at how positively he had reacted to Angel. She looked almost ready to cry. I felt the same amazement as I watched this little crippled boy and Angel connect on a level that only they seemed to fully understand.

I was very satisfied with Angel's first show experience, not because she did outstanding in the ring, but for what she did for a little boy who needed her.

This is the kind of miracle that many of us get to see when our special little horses interact with people like Brad, the elderly or others who are in need of that special connection. My husband and I feel privileged to make available all of our horses, including Angel, to those who can benefit from meeting them. It always feels like the best show in town!

Angel.

It Was a Dark and Stormy Night...

By Jody Chenoweth
Chenterra Farm Miniature Horses
Leavenworth, Kansas
www.smallhorse.com/farm/chenterra

Huge, black, ominous-looking clouds hung low on the southern horizon and the wind was starting to pick up as I charged out of the house and made my way down the hill to our bottom pasture. The evening news had just issued a tornado watch for the adjacent county and, living in Kansas as we do, we don't mess around when we hear the word tornado!

Whooping and hollering, I soon had our small herd of miniature horses rounded up and headed for the basement barn. After shutting them in, I did a head count. Belle, our little red pinto mare, wasn't with them! I raced back down to the pasture to look for her. It hadn't started to rain yet, but long, jagged flashes of lightning followed by the non-stop rumbling of thunder was getting closer and closer.

I found Belle stretched out in the tall brown grass. I got her to her feet, quickly checked her out and then felt her bag. It had really filled up since morning—hot and tight and hard. She tried to lie down again. "Oh no, Belle!" I yelled above the roar of the wind. "You can't foal now! You aren't due for another week!" Suddenly it became very still. Last year's tall brown grass had stopped its frantic rustling, and the thunder and lightning had abruptly ceased. The sky had taken on an eerie, greenish cast.

"Come on, Belle! Let's get out of here!" I screamed. I grabbed her mane and half led, half dragged her back to the foaling shed. Once inside she immediately dropped and rolled, got up, walked around and around the stall and then dropped down and rolled again. No contractions, no sweat—just up and down, walk around and around and then back down to roll again. I ran for the house to alert my husband, Fred, of a coming foal. We got a lantern, flashlight, some towels and our foaling kit and headed back to the shed. We scrubbed up and did a quick exam. Foal seemed positioned right. Everything was going to be OK. Now we just had to wait. It was close to eight o'clock. Rain mixed with hail started pelting the tin roof of the shed.

Sirens started wailing as Belle dropped and stayed down. She went into hard labor. The bubble came out and broke. Then a tiny foot appeared, and another with the nose in between. Fred and I breathed a sigh of relief. But after more straining the foal didn't slide out any further. Belle sat up on her haunches and then slowly stood up. Now we could see the problem. The nose, two front feet *and* a hind foot were all coming out at the same time. We broke the bubble and cleared the foal's nostrils. Belle dropped back into the straw. We scrubbed up again and tried to push the foal back in and to reposition the hind foot. No luck. Fred ran back through the driving rain and wind and called our vet's emergency number.

When she answered, she yelled, "Can't come. Take cover! A tornado is heading your way!" Later Fred told me that the TV was blaring "a tornado has been sighted on the ground near Jarbalo." (We live two miles east of Jarbalo.) He stayed at the phone trying to get a hold of another vet.

Back in the shed, the wind had taken part of the tin roof off. Rain poured in. I grabbed Belle's mane and tail and slid her to a drier spot. The wind was really roaring now and bending trees almost to the ground. The tin on the part of the roof that hadn't blown off was banging up and down. Belle was frightened and so was I. I dropped down on my knees beside her and pulled her head into my lap.

"Don't worry, Belle, I won't leave you! We'll go over the rainbow together." She was in hard labor now, gritting her teeth and making a horrible, loud, in-and-out gasping sound. Her eyes were glazed and staring. I started screaming for Fred but he was still in the house waiting for one of four vets he had called to get back with him. They never did.

A voice came to me, "Do something, you idiot, don't just sit there!" I jumped up, found a towel and grabbed the little foal's two front legs with one hand and the rear one with the other. Each time Belle had a contraction, I pulled down and in an arc. I pulled and I pulled but the foal wouldn't budge. My arms were getting weak and shaking.

Original watercolor by Jody Chenoweth.

I kept screaming, "Help! Help us! Somebody help us! Please, God, help me to help little Belle." My strength returned and I pulled—again and again and again. And then with one final pull, the baby plopped out—placenta and all. Outside everything became very hushed again. The rain had stopped, the wind was no longer howling, the tin on the roof had stopped banging and I was no longer screaming. My legs got rubbery and I fell to the ground, landing between Belle and her baby. I remember, in the eerie golden light of the lantern, how beautiful everything looked.

Belle and her baby were stretched full out on their sides looking so peaceful. I ran my hand over Belle's flank. It was warm and wet and was slowly, almost imperceptibly, going in and out. She was still alive! But the foal? It wasn't breathing—no heartbeat—just a wet, bloody, little black and white lifeless lump. I again made sure the baby's nostrils were clear, jumped up, grabbed the hind legs and swung the foal upside down in an arc. Back and forth, back and forth. I finally let it go and it slithered back down into the straw—a limp, lifeless lump.

"Not now, baby," I whispered. "You are not going to give up on me now!" Just that morning I had read an article, "How to give CPR to foals." I pinched one nostril shut and blew gently into the other one. I then put my palms over the heart area behind the left leg and "pumped" five times. Then I blew in the nose again. Over and over I did this and finally I felt it—a faint heartbeat!

But the baby wasn't breathing right. I grabbed a straw and poked it up one of its nostrils. It coughed and began taking big deep breaths. I started to cry and dropped down on the wet straw beside this precious, new little life. I broke the tough, stretchy cord and with a towel rubbed the short curly little hair, until it was almost dry, all the while repeating, over and over again, "Thank you, God." Belle never looked up.

Chenterra Dixie Darlin'.

Although it had seemed an eternity, all of the above happened within ten minutes. I heard Fred yelling that he couldn't get a vet. He walked into the shed and saw the foal trying to get to its feet and his mouth dropped open. "I don't believe it," he said. "How did you get it out?"

"It" was a black and white pinto filly. We named her Chenterra Dixie Darlin'. Our vet came out the next morning and discovered that Belle had a big hematoma in the lining of her vagina and Dixie would probably always limp on her near hind leg because I had stretched a cruciate ligament while pulling her out. But that was OK. We were all three alive and well.

Dixie was Belle's first foal and at first Belle wouldn't have anything to do with her. She flattened her ears and kicked at that little thing that had caused her so much pain. We separated them, milked Belle out and fed Dixie with a baby bottle for three days. Then suddenly, Belle's maternal instincts kicked in and she became a very good mama.

I will never forget that dark and stormy night back in the spring of '93 when a small miracle happened in an old foaling barn. The tornado had done a lot of damage around our area but had skirted our farm. Maybe it wasn't a miracle after all—perhaps it just wasn't the right time for an old lady, a sweet little mini mare and her baby to check out the land of Oz.

Too Much Information

By Penny Lary
Patty Cake Ranch
Dallas, Texas
www.pattycakeranch.com

Years ago when my youngest daughter, Melanie, was just starting third grade, I volunteered to bring a miniature horse to her home room for Show and Tell.

She was attending a large public grade school in the heart of North Dallas, with quite a diverse student body. I imagined it would be a rare opportunity for many of the children to see a real horse up close.

I arrived at school at the appointed time and parked my trailer in the circle driveway out front. Many of the classrooms had windows overlooking the driveway. Little faces began to appear at several of the windows as I opened the back gate of the big trailer and offloaded my little colt.

I led the little guy, barely taller than my knee, down the hall past the principal's office and into Mel's classroom. Already assembled was the entire third grade, all four sections of children, with all their teachers. Although the kids were amazed and excited, they stayed pretty calm for seven- and eight-year-olds.

My colt and I took our place in the center of the room. We had everyone's undivided attention.

I captivated the audience as I entertained and educated the kids on the wonders of the miniature horse. After about 15 minutes (they're eight, remember?), I asked if anyone had any questions. A hand shot up from the back row as a surprisingly mature-looking young man asked without hesitation:

"What's that thang hangin' down on that horse?"

There was no mistaking it. I'd heard him all right. As my life was passing before me while simultaneously looking into the startled eyes of all four sections of homeroom teachers, I asked the kid to repeat the question.

Think, dammit, think.

"What's that long thang hangin' down there?"

Had I been alone with my own children, or perhaps those of close friends whose value systems weren't wholly unknown to me, I might have answered by giving the precise clinical and biological explanation. But was I completely free to do that for total strangers? Eight-year-old strangers?

I decided I wasn't. But I didn't want to completely cop out either. Storks don't bring these babies to my house. I don't gather them out of the cabbage patch. I swallowed silently and plunged ahead.

"This is a little boy horse. You know there are males and females in all species of animals, and this is a male. So since he's a little boy horse, he'll look different from a little girl horse. He has what's called male genitalia."

"Understand?"

"Oh," says the kid, "I thought it was called a lead rope."

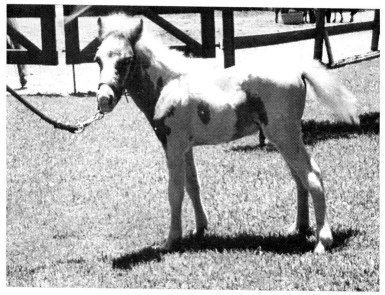

A mini colt goes to school.

An End, and a Beginning

By Jenny Hudson
Lil Tykes Miniature Horse Farm
Flint, Texas
http://www.geocities.com/liltykesminis/

Calendar notation: *July 17, 1995. Fire! Everything is gone!*

Sometimes a thing will happen that seems so bad at the time, we cannot imagine anything good ever coming of it. I didn't know that out of the tragedy that befell my family in July of 1995, my whole life would change for the better.

We live in a beautifully wooded, rural area outside Tyler, Texas. One hot, dry July day our neighbor decided to burn some brush. Soon, his brush fire had grown and began burning out of control. It quickly crossed over to our property, gathering momentum as it engulfed everything in its path.

My husband, Jason, our two boys Brannon and Brice, and I were not at home at the time. We are grateful to God for that. But our beautiful home, built entirely of wood, burned to the ground within minutes. We lost our house and everything in it.

Fortunately my parents live close by, and we were able to move in with them.

At first my attention was focused on the business of rebuilding our lives. The boys started school and we all tried to make the best of the situation. But as the weeks and months went by, I began to feel very depressed. It was difficult for the boys to find a quiet place to do homework. My days were so long trying to deal with all the decisions and pressures. At night I was often too tired and stressed out to get much sleep. Privacy was non-existent.

Things continued to get worse instead of better. I couldn't stop thinking that my husband and I had lost everything material we had ever worked for. Then I began having panic attacks. I was frightened something else really bad would happen to us and maybe this time we wouldn't escape. I couldn't seem to snap myself out of the fear I was feeling.

Looking back I think I must have been having a kind of post-traumatic distress, but at the time I couldn't see that such a reaction would have been perfectly normal. At the time, I just didn't know how I could continue coping, and that made me feel even worse.

Firecracker.

This went on for almost ten months while our new home was being built. Then one day my sister, Crissy, telephoned. A friend of hers had stopped by to show her something he had purchased. It was a miniature mare with her six-month-old filly. Crissy wondered if I wanted to come over and see them.

I have loved horses for as long as I can remember. As a kid I'd had big horses of my own, but as an adult with a family I hadn't been around a horse for over ten years. I'd heard about miniature horses, but had never seen one. I just had to go over immediately!

When I arrived at my sister's place, I saw something that would snap me out of my depression, and change my life forever. I saw this tiny sorrel and white pinto filly, as soft and fuzzy and precious as a teddy bear, with the curliest white mane and tail I had ever seen. It was absolutely love at first sight!

Crissy's friend asked if we'd be interested in purchasing the filly. My dad volunteered to buy her as a gift for the grandkids. But Dad must have known she was really for me. We named her Firecracker, and she literally lit up my life.

I began looking forward to getting up each day and doing whatever I had to do, because I knew that each day I could also spend time with Firecracker. I loved her so much, and she returned that love. Whenever she saw me coming, she'd run toward me, whinnying softly. My depression lifted and my panic attacks stopped.

Today Firecracker is a lovely, brightly-colored red and white mare with babies of her own. She has 15 other AMHA miniature horse friends who live at our home.

And we could not imagine living life without them.

Two Little Angels
for the Golden Lady

Golden Lady came one day, from a place so far alone
With a face of innocence, alert, but uncertain, her journey began
Somewhere, in those big walnut eyes, lay a heart full of love
Her golden coat so long and thick lay warm against her sides
The mane so full, like fluffy snow, streamed down
    her neck and face
Dark curls hung down around her hooves covering signs of time
The gentle little one stood quiet that day, as the blacksmith
    trimmed her feet
Away she looked, who are these people? What is
    my destiny today?
Unsure, but willing, she followed her new friend home
    across the icy paths
The sun danced bright against the bluest of skies
    and glistened on the snow
Friends she found, small and large horses, nickered
    and sniffed the air
Today, she could start to find peace in her warm barn
    filled with love
Lady's new friend remembered someone that wanted a little horse
A little horse for two very special little girls, what a great idea!
Excited and sure this would be a match made in heaven,
    the search began
Sounds perfect, Mom said, so gentle and mature,
    so small and strong
Pictures were sent, calls were made, days passed so slowly
    for the girls
Surely today we can see little Lady, but time it was not,
    so pictures must do

Dad made ready for the Lady, the girls checked to be sure
    it was just right
Time had been set, arrangements were made, hearts
    swelled with excitement
The day had come, warmest in weeks,
    the girls could wait no more
The journey was long, two hours passed like twenty,
    but they finally arrived
There were the orange gates from the pictures,
    and the little horses they saw
So this is the place where Lady had played,
    the place we had yearned to see
Prayers do get answered, blessings do come,
    hearts were filled with joy
Lucky I guess, blessed I know, are the children who care
    for God's creatures
The smell of the barn, the sound of munching hay,
    their soft winter coat
A warm muzzle against your neck, the eyes that follow your steps
The understanding in their heart, knowing you love them
These are parts of the friendship and devotion that come
    with a horse
This is the answer to dreams, the key to a whole new day
The beginning of memories that will last a lifetime
This is the day two little angels take home the Golden Lady
Take care of her and love her every day
She will take care of you and love you forever!

By Connie D. Ballard
Cherokee Stables
New Lebanon, Ohio
www.cherokeestables.com

Beethoven

By Dona Neargarder
Kickapoo Acres
Fletcher, Ohio
http://kickapoo-acres.virtualave.net

"Beethoven" was the result of an accidental breeding between a full brother and sister. He was a tiny 14" with the biggest blue eyes when born, but it was obvious from the very beginning that he was a dwarf. He had the trademark bulbous head, large eyes, high-set nostrils, undershot jaw and leg deviations. Most of his dwarf characteristics were very slight, except for the leg deviations in the rear. His fetlock joints were so lax that his hooves turned completely under, forcing him to stand on the end of his cannon bone. Our vet tried splinting his legs first. Of course, after a few weeks of this, we saw that it just was not working. Our vet knew by this time how much we loved this little guy and were willing to do anything that we could to give him the best healthy life possible. So, he recommended that we take him to Ohio State Vet College and have him evaluated for leg surgery. We did that and he was accepted. The surgeon there even said that he had seen much worse, and that this was a very commonplace surgery, done almost every day there to correct leg deviations in full-size horses. I left Beethoven and his mom there feeling much better about our decision. Went back in three days to pick him up. By that time, little Beethoven had won the hearts of all the staff, doctors, and students who had come in contact with him, and they all hated to see him go.

Both his back legs were wrapped up tightly and the dressings had to be changed every other day and re-dressed. We were very diligent about this and Beethoven took it all in stride. We would lie him on his side on the picnic table to do this, and he would always lie very still until we were done. The surgery site looked great and was healing very well, and Beethoven was running and bucking just as if there wasn't a thing wrong with him. It really did my heart good to see that!

Then, only four days away from taking him back to OSU for evaluation and removal of the wraps, we noticed that he seemed lethargic in his stall and didn't seem to want to get up. When he did get up, he wouldn't put any weight on his leg. We had just checked his legs the morning before and they were fine, no sign of redness or infection; and he wasn't due to have his dressings removed again until the following day…but we knew something was wrong. We removed his dressings and were horrified at what we saw. Green ooze was coming from the surgery site! We quickly wrapped it back up and called the vet. We had little Beethoven lying in the grass when the vet arrived. He kept saying, "Calm down now…it can't be as bad as you say, if it was OK yesterday." We unwrapped his leg to show the ooze and putrid smell, and our vet (who is an equine specialist and whom I trust explicitly) got a horrified look on his face and said, "Oh my God, Dona…we are going to have to put him down."

It turned out that Beethoven wasn't doing as well as he looked. He had been harboring a "systemic infection" from the surgery, that eventually cut off the blood supply to his leg, and of course, the leg "died." It was like a limp noodle. I can't even begin to explain the helplessness my husband and I felt at that point. We both bawled like babies when Beethoven was put to sleep (while still lying there on his side, munching on grass). Our very kind vet was shedding a few tears also.

Beethoven.

I still don't regret giving this little guy a chance though; chances are that if he hadn't developed the infection, he would have gone on to live many healthy years. We must remember—as "breeders," we are the ones who have bred these little horses down over the years, we are the ones who have confused the genes, we are the ones who are responsible for bringing these little lives into this world, and we should give them every chance possible to have a healthy, pain-free life. We should also have the responsibility to know when that isn't possible, and spare them unnecessary pain by putting them to rest. I will never be ashamed of producing a dwarf, as it is one of those things that is almost impossible to predict. And, truth be known, the dwarf gene probably runs in most all Miniature bloodlines.

Dwarfs have the most lovable, sweet personalities that I've ever encountered, and they make the *best* pets around. They *are* "high-maintenance" though, and most require extra hoof trimmings, dental work, and attention to other health problems they may have. Anyone who is contemplating buying a dwarf for a pet, should very seriously consider everything that will be involved before doing so. Extra work, extra expense, etc. (and possible heartache down the road!). These "little loves" deserve the best homes possible where people are willing and able to provide, not only the love, but all the necessary attention to their health problems.

A Diamond in the Rough

By Emily Conder
Conder Minis
New Smyrna Beach, Florida

I thought I'd share this with all you horse lovers out there. I love miniatures, and love showing them, and whenever I get the opportunity to look at some possible purchase or just to see what's out there, I take it. I like to go to sales just to see what horses are bringing and see what's there, so when I heard there was going to be a sale just for miniatures, I took the opportunity to go.

It was in the middle of May 1999, and the sale was in Ocala, Florida, just about one and a half hours from where I live. There weren't many miniatures there, and a few ponies. I was walking down all the aisles just checking the horses out. I came to the last aisle and at the end was a woman holding a little bay mini. It looked like a living skeleton, head hung low, and back leg rested. So I approached the woman and asked how old the horse was and if it was a mare, stallion or gelding. It was a three-year-old bay mare, although she looked like a standing skeleton. It was terrible; she had no spirit, no life. I knew I had to do something. I went and found my parents and brought them to her. They were in shock. How could someone let a horse get this skinny? The lady holding her acted like nothing was wrong. I would have been too embarrassed to have that horse in public knowing I did this to it!

My parents and I went to the sale ring and waited for her to go through, and when she did, the lady didn't get enough money for her, so we immediately followed her back to her stall. My parents worked out a deal to buy her and two others. The other two mares weren't near as bad as the bay mare, but still very skinny. As we walked them out to the trailer, I had to go at a snail's pace to let the bay mare keep up with me. When we got to the trailer we had to lift her in, being we don't have a ramp.

Sweetwaters Little Fancy Girl—Before.

When we got home, we helped the mare get off the trailer and I walked her to a stall. We put the others out in a pasture but the bay mare was far too weak to go out in the pasture with the other two. When I put her in her stall, she was so tired she just stood in the same spot I put her. I guess the walk took all her energy. That day we wormed her and gave her shots. We were worried the wormer might make her sick because she was so skinny, but we had no choice; all we could do at this point was hope she'd make it.

The next day we turned her out in a small paddock. All she did was stand in the same corner all day. She was so skinny, I could grab her hip bones with my whole hand. You could see her ribs from far away. She couldn't even lift her head or shut her mouth all the way, and you could count all the bones in her body. I have seen a lot of skinny horses in my life, but none on the same level as this one.

After a few days, we decided to move her to an old dog pen with a covered area. It was perfect for her and she loved it. As the days passed, she got better and better, and after about two weeks we put her in a stall again and turned her out during the day time. She was finally getting back some life, and when the other horses got to running around next to her, she'd actually lift her tail and prance around. Surprisingly, she was gaining weight rather fast, and as her weight got better so did her energy level and coat. Slowly I started teaching her stuff like bathing, tying, etc.

After two months of good food and grooming, she was a different horse. When I first bought her it was with no intentions of future showing plans at the time, but now she had life again and had turned into one of my favorites. Slowly I started training her how to lunge and set up for halter, even ground drive, and about three to four months after we bought her, I started working her for halter. But then it happened; she cut her right eye and had to go to rest for about a month. It just figures; finally I get her back to good health, and boom! Now this.

My plans for showing her at the 1999 Mini-O-Rama at that point went away. But about one month before Mini-O-Rama, her eye looked way better, so I started working her again.

In November 1999, I took her to her first show ever, just six months after I bought her. She was a totally different horse, and she stood Grand Champion Senior Mare! Wow! Just six months after I bought her!

The next weekend I took her to the Sunshine Classic and she stood Grand Champion Senior Mare again! No one could believe this was the same horse in the pictures I had. Now she is one of my top show horses. Who would have guessed that I could do this with the bag of bones I had just six months ago.

This just goes to show you that there are many "diamonds in the rough" out there. I honestly believe that if it wasn't for us, this horse, Sweetwaters Little Fancy Girl, would not even be alive right now. If I ever see a horse in need, I will take the chance to help it, and I encourage you to do the same. There are so many great horses out there like her that need that second chance at life. I am proud to say that she will go to Eastern Regionals and Nationals, and she will have a lifelong home here at Conder Minis.

Sweetwaters
Little Fancy
Girl—After.

Postscript: Sweetwaters Little Fancy Girl won Youth 7-and-Under Senior Mare National Champion and also High Point in the nation for Youth 13-17 Senior Mare!

Mr. Mom

By Jeri Hix
Li'l Dudes Miniature Horses
Farmersville, Ohio

A couple of years ago, I bought a colt, Jammer, that wasn't weaned when I purchased him. Since I was only about five miles away from this farm, and knew the people pretty well, I asked if I could bring the mare home with my colt and wean him here. I was just so anxious to get my little guy home, I didn't want to wait. I had not had any mini babies of my own yet and didn't want to miss out on this stage of his life. They agreed to let me do this, but told me they would have to have the mare back by a certain date.

Well, there was a misunderstanding on my part about how long I could keep the mare, so of course they called and wanted me to bring the mare back so they could rebreed and sell her. Needless to say, I had not even started the weaning process! So I loaded the mare up with my little Jammer screaming his head off and running all over the place. It broke my heart as I pulled down the road with him screaming and mom screaming back! Talk about a guilt trip! I punished myself all the way there and back.

When I returned home about 45 minutes later, little Jammer was still running, screaming and having fits! It upset me so badly, I didn't know what to do. Finally I thought, I'm going to try putting him in with my gelding; every one of my horses gets along with Ghost.

I led Ghost into the paddock, and Jammer ran up to him and started sniffing. From that moment on, my little gelding Ghost became "Mr. Mom" to Jammer. It amazed me how protective Ghost was of Jammer. Where you saw Jammer, you always saw Ghost. As time went by, if any of my other horses came near Jammer, Ghost would intervene.

They slept side by side, sunbathed together, ate together, played together. I was constantly amazed at the bonding they shared.

Well, it's two years later and my little Jammer started breeding my mares this spring. I was so afraid he would get studdish and be mean to Ghost. But nope, Ghost is still his Mr. Mom; they are still stalled together and turned out *always* together or there is heck to pay. I took Ghost to the County Fair the other night and Jammer got so mad! He screams every time I separate them...except when I take Jammer out to breed a mare!

Ghost and Jammer.

Little Icarus

By Erin McCloy
EM's Miniature Horses
Birdsboro, Pennsylvania

EM's Miniature Horses began late in the summer of 1998 when I purchased a small colt from a local breeder. The colt was adorable—a little brown ball of fluff with a long snow-white mane and tail. He was only three months old the day I brought him home…little did I know that he was only going to be with us for a few months more.

Erin's Kid Icarus, or "Iggy," was my very first horse, let alone miniature horse. I had a few years of experience with the standard-sized animal, but never such a small one…26" to be exact. Iggy ended up being raised more like a dog than an equine. He was given free rein of the yard, rarely ever was he penned, and he was occasionally allowed in the house. He even had a little stuffed monkey to sleep with that would squeak whenever he'd play with it. But most of all, he loved to run with the dogs.

Icarus caught on to the halter thing rather quickly but didn't like to be led around. He loved his freedom more than I will ever be able to appreciate…but he loved me even more. I was a "horse" to him just like he was a friend to me. Every day, when walking home from the bus stop, I would call out his name and I would get a heartwarming whinny in return. Then he would prance around his little field until I would come to visit him. But he still did prefer to run loose with the dogs, no matter how much I pleaded with my family to keep him in the pasture. I knew that such freedom for a small horse couldn't be good and that something would eventually happen…after all, we do live in the middle of the woods and hunting season is popular in this area…and my little brown fluff-ball did look very much like a deer. I was wrong about what would happen, though.

One muddy afternoon around 5:00 p.m., during one of Iggy's favorite running sessions, he slipped and fell. Icarus slid head first into a stone fire pit, breaking his neck on impact. I saw it all and no matter how loud I screamed for help, nothing would have helped my friend then. That night, I lost my one true love and my very best friend. Iggy showed me what it was like to have my very own pet to love and to train, to care for and to actually be responsible for. It was very hard for me to let him go that cold February evening, but I knew I had to. I took Icarus' death very hard and I still occasionally find myself crying at night with a little bit of his tail entangled around my fingers. But I know he is still with me even though I can't see him in the flesh. His spirit is here, guiding me always and I will meet up with him again…someday.

Icarus won first prize
in the Halloween Costume Contest.

◊ Erin's Kid Icarus ◊

May 21st, 1998 – February 5th, 1999

"He had barely begun to live…"

The Paws That Refreshed

By Mary Papenhausen
Nortonville, Kansas

No matter how cold a day starts out or ends, we must continue with the daily chores that revolve around our "little ones"—those cute little fuzzy four-legged critters that insist on eating and drinking at least twice a day. Actually, it's a good thing they *do* insist on that daily attention, because it forces me to get up and out. At least get the old blood flowing a little bit at some point in the long days we've had to face here lately.

Now my mornings usually go the same way every day. I get out to the shop where I am greeted by a fairly large, orange and white cat who chose to adopt us after being chased away from his original home by a very large dog. His name is Chester. After Chester gets his food and de-iced water, it's on to say "Hi" to our two stars, miniature horses Shortie and Dillon. They reside in their own personal stalls out in back of the shop. They spend their evenings in their spacious rooms with wind shelter, shavings, food and water—not to mention occasional piped-in music when I forget to turn the radio off.

I greet them with hugs and pats, words of encouragement, and a tiny bit of oats. Oh, they are so happy to see me! They even try to help me pour those oats into their feed boxes! I guess I am too slow for them. Ha!

My next step is emptying the blocks of ice in their water buckets and replacing it with a drinkable liquid. This I place outside with plenty of hay to help them cope with the cold day ahead.

When they have finished eating their grain, I turn Shortie out in one section of pasture; then little Dillon to his special little corner of the world. They exchange a few choice nips and a little buck or two, then, with the fence between them, they settle down for a tasty breakfast of hay.

By this time, all of my gear—the coveralls, scarf, boots, earmuffs and gloves—are starting to have a little trouble keeping the cold out. But nevertheless, duty calls and it is off to get the wheelbarrow and rake. Not only has the water turned to bricks but so have the little piles so strategically placed around Shortie's and Dillon's stalls. They do such good work! It comes from practice, you know!

I start with Shortie's stall, flipping those little clunkers into the wheelbarrow after sifting them out of the shavings. When finished, I continue over to Dillon's domain to find…no deposits in sight! At first I was startled! Could Dillon be sick? I looked a little closer and noticed a numerous amount of shavings scooped up into great mounds all over his stall. It looked like a cat convention had been there! When I got closer with the rake for a further inspection, I realized that good ol' Chester had decided to help me with this tedious chore. He had gone around and covered up all those frozen little piles just for me! That must have been quite an undertaking for the little guy!

Well, it sure gave me a good chuckle and it makes me feel pretty special. After all, who else has four-legged help cleaning up a mess created by another four-legged creature? But despite Chester's help, I still had to find "them" all and dispose of "them" in the usual way. Hmmm…I wonder if I could teach Chester to put "them" in the wheelbarrow?

A Friendship Trilogy

(A Miniature Horse Friendship from Three Perspectives)

Making Friends

By Nona Lacy (age 31)
Little Lacy's Miniature Horse Farm
McLouth, Kansas

In May of 1999, my family moved to northeastern Kansas for my husband to begin a new job. Although we were very happy to be in this new job, I was very lonely as it takes me a long time to make new friends. I was still trying to find my place when my mom called to tell me she was coming for a visit in June. I was so excited and I began to plan some fun things for us to do while she visited. I planned trips to local museums and places of interest and began to prepare for her trip to my new home. My parents were getting ready to retire and were very excitedly planning to raise miniature horses. I had heard about the little horses, but being a full-size horse person all my life, I had little interest in them. After all, what were they good for?

I continued to prepare and I went to the grocery store for a few last-minute items. The store I stopped at that day was not my usual shopping spot, but it was closest to the area that I was in. As I finished my shopping, I began to drive out of the parking lot. I came up behind a large vehicle and noticed some etching on the back windows. It said, "Serenity Acres Miniature Horse Farm." I immediately thought how great it would be to take my mom to a miniature horse farm while she was visiting. Although she had made a lot of plans for their farm, she had not yet actually had a chance to spend any time with actual miniatures. I tried to attract the attention of the driver of the vehicle, but with no luck. I committed the name to memory and headed home, determined I would call on the phone and try to set up an appointment.

Left to Right: Jody Chenoweth,
Sandy Martin, and Nona Lacy.
Photo by Lowell L. Martin 2000.

I was very disappointed when I arrived at home to find that the farm name was not listed anywhere in the phone book. I turned next to any other stable in the area that might be able to give me some information. I called the nearest stable and explained what I was looking for. What luck! The stable I called just happened to know the exact farm I was looking for. In fact, they had actually boarded some of their horses in the past. The owner of the stables was happy to provide me with the name and number of the owner of the miniature horse farm. I called her next. The woman I contacted was Sandy Martin. I felt a little apprehensive about asking to come over to see her horses. Little did I know that total strangers stopping to see these little guys is nothing new to a miniature horse owner!

Of course, she was totally agreeable to us visiting her farm and I scheduled an afternoon for us to visit. When my mother and I arrived at Serenity Acres, I never expected to be so taken with the little creatures that I was to encounter. We had a wonderful visit and as we talked about these sweet little animals and they were pushing up all around me, I fell in love. It didn't take me very long to realize that I wanted to be a part of the miniature horse scene. I noticed quickly that Sandy had her hands full with 20-plus little horses and little (no pun intended) help.

A few weeks after our visit to the farm, my mom left, but I still could not stop thinking about the little horses and the very kind woman I had met. I wrote her a letter proposing a plan. I offered to help her around the farm in exchange for information and knowledge, anything, that would aid my parents and my miniature horse beginnings. She was hesitant to accept the offer, but did. I began to help her out doing odds and ends around the farm. I quickly became attached to many of the horses. I gained more and more knowledge and soon began to meet other miniature horse owners, who also very generously shared all they knew about the little ones. I also obtained my first horse from Serenity Acres, as more were to follow later.

However, the best thing I came away with was many new friends. Sandy and I hit it off immediately and began to spend more and more time together. We, along with another person, Jody Chenoweth, began to visit other miniature horse farms and spending time together. Despite our age differences, we became the best of friends. We took every opportunity to jump in the car and go see horses (or whatever else we decided needed seeing). We had many wonderful times together. They became truly good friends, who were there for me through good and bad times. I have since moved from Kansas, but we continue to be friends over the miles. So I have another wonderful reason to love those little horses. Not only have they provided companionship for me, but also they were the very thing that helped me create relationships that changed my life forever.

The Little Ties That Bind

By Sandy Martin (age 61)
Serenity Acres Miniature Horse Farm
Leavenworth, Kansas
http://serenityacre.com

Our long-suffering husbands just sighed and said, "Have fun, dear," knowing that when the three of us "girls" got together it would be anyone's guess when we'd show up back home! And off we'd go for a few hours of pure and simple visiting, and horse-related activities. Every little diner in every little neighboring town knew that we'd be there awhile, we'd be so busy talking we'd forget to order! No one owning a miniature horse was safe from us; we scheduled "farm tours" on the spur of the moment, we went to parades, nursing homes, schools, sanctioned shows and fun matches, club meetings, committee meetings, TV stations, radio stations, vet clinics, driving clinics and clipping clinics. There were BBQs, stamping parties, farewell parties, birthday parties...did I mention parades? We'd even visit each other's farms to see the latest foals, newest mares, greatest auction finds or newest barn improvements. Or someone would just bring a dinner to the one of us who was sick, a phone call to see "what's up," or a horse-sitting stint for whoever was out of town.

But we each have a life, too. One of us is an RN, mother of two active youngsters and minister's wife; one of us is a well-traveled, retired Army wife and grandmother of a teenager; and one of us is a great-grandmother, artist and farm wife. What, you ask, would create such a tight bond between three women ranging in ages from 31 years to 61 years to 71 years and with such diverse backgrounds? What, you ask, are miniature horses good for? This wonderful little animal is the cement that has bonded a beautiful friendship that will live in each of our hearts long after life's events have separated us!

The Three Amigos

By Jody Chenoweth (age 71)
Chenterra Farm
Leavenworth Kansas
www.smallhorse.com/farms.chenterra

Good friends and good horses–who can ask more of life?

—William McIntire

Sometimes, if you are *very* lucky, God sends people into your life who make it more meaningful and more beautiful.

I first met Sandy Martin in 1993 when she came to our farm to buy a couple of mini broodmares. She told me she loved horses, but had been hurt when thrown from her Quarter Horse mare and didn't want to ride anymore. Raising Miniature Horses seemed to be the perfect answer.

Sandy was middle-aged, pretty and proper, and although not frail-looking, she appeared soft and not used to hard work. I remember the twinkle in her eye as I handed her the lead ropes of the two mini mares she had picked out, Jelly Bean and Nakita. I also remember thinking, "This gal will never last in the miniature horse business."

Wrong!

Sandy Martin was, in fact, an army brat, tough and tenacious—two qualities I feel you need if you are going to breed miniature horses. She jumped right into it and learned the hard way about unscrupulous sellers and the risks of buying blindly at auctions. She learned about dystocia and how to assist mares with foaling problems. She learned to recognize good conformation; she learned about feeding, grooming and showing, and soon had a National Top Ten stallion. Never embarrassed to ask questions or to learn from her mistakes, she has become a successful and knowledgeable breeder of Miniature Horses.

At first, we just talked on the phone—a lot! It seemed that every day Sandy had a question about minis. Having had horses for over 60 years, I know a lot about them, but found out how true the old say-ing is, "You never know everything there is to know about horses." Questions she'd ask that I couldn't answer I would look up–if it was a medical problem, I'd look in my Merck Vet book; if a color ques-tion, I'd check out Sponenberg; pedigrees and "what did *so and so* look like?" I'd look through my old Miniature Horse World maga-zines. So her questions had a double benefit–the more questions she asked, the more we both learned.

And with her bulldog tenacity, Sandy bugged and bugged me to get my mini cartoon book, "The Small Side," published (which I finally did). She even went with me to make sure they did it right. Her name is on the dedication page.

What I am most in awe of is that Sandy has learned to back a horse trailer! It is something I still can't do. (I accuse her of putting a testosterone patch on when she hooks her trailer up as I am convinced that being able to back a trailer is a guy thing.)

In 1999, Sandy introduced me to Nona Lacy. Young, pretty and a talented artist and songwriter, Nona is one of those quintessential "horse nuts" just like Sandy and me. We hit it off right away. She has that special horse whisperer's way with horses. Even the most cantan-kerous horse becomes docile and trusting after a few lessons in Nona's round pen.

That old horseman's saying, "I never met a person I didn't like, that likes horses" should be changed to "I never met a person I didn't like, that horses like." Horses *like* Nona.

Since the three of us lived within a stone's throw of each other, we soon became great friends and Sandy dubbed us "The Three Amigos." What a combination! On the outside, youth, middle age and old age–yet on the inside, we have so much in common that the age difference doesn't seem to matter. Oh, the fun we have had taking our minis to parades, nursing homes, clinics and fun matches. We live, breathe, talk and love horses. Especially miniature horses.

It is so reassuring to know that when I need help and can't get a vet that one or both of "mi amigas" will be there in minutes. How lucky I am to have two such good friends.

(Sad to relate, but Nona and her horses recently moved to Ari-zona. Sandy and I carry on, but it is just not the same without the third Amigo.)

The Road Song of the Three Amigos
By Jody Chenoweth

"No More–That's All"

I bought a little mini mare,
Gave her lots of tender care.
One little mini in a great big stall,
I said, "No more–that's all!"

She was lonesome so I got
Her a friend–his name was Spot.
Two little minis in a great big stall,
I said, "No more–that's all!"

Come next spring they had a filly,
Cute little thing–I named her Millie.
Three little minis in a great big stall,
I said, "No more–that's all!"

Got an offer through the mail,
Small black mare with a snow-white tail.
Four little minis in a great big stall,
I said, "No more–that's all."

Saw an ad for a pretty roan,
Went to the bank and got a loan.
Five little minis in a great big stall,
I said, "No more–that's all!"

I have never been so happy,
I just bought a leopard appy!
Six little minis in a great big stall,
I said, "No more–that's all!"

My friend gave me her old stud,
He turned out to be a dud.
Seven little minis in a great big stall,
I said, "No more–that's all!"

Pleasure driving sure looks fun,
Found a cart and a lineback dun.
Eight little minis in a great big stall,
I said, "No more–that's all!"

Then came my overo craze,
Found a frame with a crooked blaze.
Nine little minis in a great big stall,
I said, "No more–that's all!"

I scraped up some extra dough,
Bought a mare that I could show.
Ten little minis in a great big stall,
I said, "No more–that's all!"

Spot and the mares all had a fling,
Lots of babies due next spring!
Where'll I put 'em all? Oh darn!
Need more stalls and a bigger barn!

The Snowfest Parade

By Kim Sterchi
Sierra Ranch
Grass Valley, California
SierraMinis@aol.com

Steve and I attended the Snowfest Parades on March 5 and 6 and really had a great time. We left early Friday with double blankets and hoods on Bronco and his daughter Impressive. It was cold and there was snow everywhere! We backed the trailer right up to our door at the motel and after we got everything settled, I took the horses out to explore the wonder of snow for the first time. You should have seen these California horses playing, jumping and looking like "Bambi" when he first experienced ice!

We bedded the horses down for the night with three blankets each and piles of shavings. Saturday morning was cold, and on our way to Tahoe, we were worried it would be too cold for the horses without their blankets.

Upon arrival at the parade sight, the sun came out and everything warmed up. We couldn't have asked for better weather. We were asked to go next to last—right in front of the Budweiser Clydesdales. In front of us was a box of crayons. Yes, you read that right. Approximately 30 small children, each dressed up as a different color crayon. They were adorable. All of the parade entries were wonderful and everyone was so friendly. As we started down the parade route, people were yelling questions faster than we could answer them. The crowd was really excited. Suddenly, a small child broke from the crowd. He ran straight for Bronco, wrapping his arms around Bronco's neck as he reached him. For a second, we were stunned, but Bronco wasn't fazed! Without any warning, several other children in the crowd and many small crayons swarmed us like a hive of bees, and both horses were completely lost in the honeycomb of children. This is while the parade is proceeding down the street, mind you! The minis weren't upset at all at the attention—I was the one having the anxiety attack!

In the excitement, none of us were thinking about the Clydesdales until we felt the pavement moving under our feet and heard the thunder of the mighty Clydes approaching us at a very rapid speed. The crowd was thick around us as I looked back to see where the enormous horses were. My heart began to pound. The magnificent team was less than ten feet behind us and their gigantic hooves were pounding the pavement as they closed the gap between us. They weren't stopping! What was wrong with them? Couldn't they see the crayons?

Several parents, realizing the enormous team behind us could crush any and all of us, started grabbing their crayons and darting for the sidelines. Some started screaming. A moment of panic filled me as I felt the thunder of the team shaking the earth. Time was out. I lunged for the sidelines, dragging Impressive and a crayon with me. Suddenly, all was quiet. I looked up to see where Steve and Bronco were. There they were, standing only inches away from the Budweiser team, Steve looking very smug and Bronco with a look that said, "One more step, big boys, and I'll bite your fetlocks!" The team was standing quietly and completely under control.

Feeling kind of foolish and a bit indignant, I passively took my place in line again. I glanced back at the two men controlling the team to give them a squalid look—and they were grinning from ear to ear. Realizing that they were having a grand time at my expense, I had to smile also. After all, the team was never out of control, and it made for quite an impressive parade with the gentle giants towering over us as we completed the parade. Next time though, I hope they lead!

The Easter Blessing

By Audette Gladney
Gladney's Miniature Horse Ranch
Bossier, Louisiana

Our first miniature horse baby was born at 1:30 a.m. Easter morning. I did not have a monitor or alarm system in the barn, I just had a clock and my two feet. I would check my mare every 20 minutes setting a timer. On this night I had gone to bed about 12:30 after preparing the boys' clothes for church the next Easter Day. I had forgotten to set the timer. I fell asleep and was awakened at 1:27 for some reason. My heart jumped with the thought that I forgot the timer for the mare. I ran to the barn and to my surprise I was just in time to save the life of my first foal. It was still in the sac on the ground, the mother standing over it. I was so scared to look and see if it was dead or alive. The sac moved and I jumped into action. The baby was small, black from head to toe, and alive!

I ran back into the house and started yelling for my family to get up and come and see the miracle in the barn. I grabbed the needed towels and other foaling supplies I had in a basket at the back door, which were ready for this blessed event, and ran back to the barn so that I would not miss any of the new foal's first steps.

My three boys were young, King was eight, David seven, and Mark was four. Tim had gotten them all up so that they could come and see the new foal. They all three came walking to the barn in their cute little PJs, hair a mess, wiping sleep from their little eyes with their tiny hands, dragging Easter baskets on the ground behind them, full of Easter surprises. Each little face as they looked at the tiny black foal, smiling from ear to ear. Mark being the smallest, smiled up at me and said, "Mom! Look, the Easter Bunny brought us a new baby." We all laughed, and because of this, the baby's name was "Gladney's Easter Spirit" ("Spirit" for short).

Mark, King, David, and Tim
with new mom Misty...and Spirit.

How I Became a Mini Owner

By Virginia Cason
Diamond "C" Miniature Horses
Brownwood, Texas
rhcasonjr@verizon.net

Dedicated in Loving Memory of my Daddy–Dudley Aldridge

I was reared on a working ranch with cattle, horses and goats. I started out at an early age going with my Daddy to work each morning, on my Shetland pony, riding with him until at least noon. In the hot summertime, I was ready to return home long before my Daddy was through roping and doctoring worms. He carried a canteen of water for us to drink and sometimes my Mom would sneak a piece of fruit in his saddlebag for me to have a snack.

With this background, I grew up riding horseback and loved nothing better. I went away to school and did not get to ride as much as I once did. I always had a horse at the ranch I could ride. In 1955 I had the honor of being "Rodeo Queen" of the Comanche Rodeo, sponsored by The Comanche National Bank. By this time, I was married and still did not have too much time for riding.

My husband and I bought six acres of land, where I raised orphan calves my Daddy gave me and Barbado sheep. This was fun and I enjoyed it until my health started deteriorating very rapidly. I was chasing one of my bucks, fell down and broke my wrist. It was downhill from there and in l993 I had five broken bones in one year. I was under the care of a physician all this time, but he wasn't getting the job done. My daughter said, "Enough, Mom," and starting looking for a specialist for me. She found a doctor in Dallas, where I had all kinds of tests and the results were that I had osteoporosis in a very bad way. I had lost over 70% of my bone structure. I was a very high risk for a broken hip. The doctor told me that at the rate I was going, I would be in a wheelchair within a year. He also stated that I could never again ride a horse. He advised me to get rid of my calves, which I did, but not my sheep.

I was deeply depressed and I am afraid I did not do a very good job of hiding it from my family. My daughter told me I could find other things to do. My Daddy knew how I felt about not ever being able to ride again. You see, Daddy was 92 at this time and still riding his horse and helping gather cows. He didn't say a whole lot about it to me, but obviously he gave it a great deal of thought.

My brother, who lived with my Daddy and ranched with him, had to be out of town for a day. Since Daddy voluntarily gave up driving at age 90, I told my brother I would come get Daddy on this day and take him out to lunch and just drive around. On the way to lunch I mentioned to Daddy that I was kind of thinking about getting Karen's (my daughter) old cart out and seeing if I could find a pony to pull the cart. I thought surely that I could do this and not get hurt. Daddy didn't say anything then and we drove on into town and had lunch. After we got back in the car, Daddy said he thought he knew where a man had some ponies if I wanted to go see them. I was immediately interested. I asked where they were and he said between Dublin and Stephenville.

We were in Comanche at the time, so off we went. The place my Daddy took me was none other than Jack Gerhart's in Dublin, Texas, the home of The Texans. Mr. Gerhart is a pioneer in the miniature horse business and he is also a third-generation breeder of miniatures. I had always wanted a miniature horse ever since I first saw one in "The Horseman." Daddy said we did not need one. I was ecstatic and fell in love with the miniature horses the minute I saw them. Daddy laughed and winked at Mr. Gerhart when I wanted him to buy me one on the spot. He said we would have to wait and see what R.H. (my husband) had to say about it.

We had a delightful visit, I was much cheered up, and pretty sure I was going to own one of those little critters before too many days. I took Daddy home, came on home to Brownwood and could not wait to tell my husband about them. Well, he came home from work and I started telling him all about the miniatures. He asked what can they do? What good are they? He stated that he didn't think we had any use for them. My heart and hopes fell. I am pretty persistent when I really want something and I really, really, did want a miniature horse. So I thought, if I could just get him to look at them I knew he would be gone–hook, line and sinker.

So I suggested we just drive over to take a look and then see what he thought. He agreed and off we went. We were there less than ten minutes when he told me to pick one out. I promptly chose a sorrel pinto stallion, four months old, by the name of "Texans Cherokee Chief." My husband wrote Mr. Gerhart a check and we came home. I was a "happy camper!"

Dudley Aldridge and Texans Cherokee Chief.

Mr. Gerhart and his daughter delivered the horse to our home, as at that time I did not have a horse trailer. That is how I got started in the miniature horse business in 1994 and have been in the business ever since. I started with one baby colt and last year at one time, we had 27 horses. Oh yes, after my husband retired, he saw how much fun showing horses and meeting all the wonderful miniature horse people was, so he joined me in the business in May 1997.

A Mini Dream

By Dona M. Brown
Brown's Mini Pets
Topeka, Kansas

This is a story about my little 31" black gelding named Shadow. Last year we made our yearly trip to our local nursing home. After we got there, the lady in charge approached us with a request from the family of a man who wasn't expected to live to bring Shadow to his window so that he might see a horse for one last time. He was a man who had raised horses. We at first tried to take Shadow close to the man's window so he could look out and see the little horse. All the flowers around his window prevented us from getting Shadow close enough for him to see. I could see the disappointment on the lady's face and suggested we take Shadow into the man's room. To her delight we started down the hallway of the home. Shadow followed dutifully along. He was calm and seemed to know that he was on his way to something important.

We reached the room and went inside. With the man's family all around, I led Shadow to the side of the man's bed. The man kept going in and out of a sleepy state as the lady kept asking him to wake up and see the little horse. Shadow seemed to sense the reason he was there and moved closer to the bed, closer to the man's hand. He kept his eyes on the man and waited patiently for the next move. The lady took the man's hand and stroked Shadow's soft nose. The man seemed to know the horse was there but quickly went back to his sleepy state. Everyone seemed content that they had made their best effort for their dad to see the horse. They snapped a few pictures and we turned and left the room. Shadow followed down the long hallway, stopping to let several curious residents take their turn to see the little horse. Today was an extra special day. We could feel good about our visit.

Dona with Shadow.

As time went on, I could only assume that the man had passed away. A year later we made our trip back to the home. Several residents were sitting in their wheelchairs waiting to see Shadow again. A gentleman was sitting tall and straight in his chair. "Remember him?" asked the lady. "He is the man Shadow and you visited in his room last year." The man immediately started petting the horse with a huge smile on his face. The man remembered a horse coming to his room and him petting it but he thought he was dreaming. A picture hanging in his room of him petting a little horse proved him wrong. The man had made it through that rough day a year ago and he and I had a nice visit about the days when he had horses. Shadow stood near by, close to the man, and the man's hand gently petted Shadow's soft nose.

Clementine

May 1, 1998 - February 13, 2000

Those shocking eyes could stop my heart
That raspy high-pitched whinny
She'd stamp her tiny golden hooves
My fragile runt-sized mini.

Her forelock billowed even more
Than God's enormous clouds
Her tail could wipe the heavens dry
Or stay unwanted crowds.

Her fur-pelt deeper than the sea
With spray to heaven splayed
We'd laugh like fools at broken rules
As my two minis played.

They'd leap and race and rear and buck
And nip and kick and roll
The other looking elegant
And she, a wizard-troll.

She'd stop and brace her magic feet
And flash those lightning eyes
Then slowly lower to my lap
I'd sing her lullabies.

Gentle as a flower's breath
Yet seeming far away
Her mystery stirred our aching hearts
And would that she could stay——

Quite like a holy spirit
Is the closest I can come
To describe the indefinable
About this little one.

Could even lift her off the ground
As once I had to do
And held her dying in my arms
Before she reached age two.

By Penelope Plumb
Deer Isle, Maine

Havenbrooks Bubby

By Linda Rodriguez
Havenbrook Miniature Horse Farm
Burkesville, Kentucky
http://www.angelfire.com/biz4/havenbrook/

In early 1999, we purchased a tiny, refined mare already in foal, never anticipating the adventure and story about to unfold. Bubby was born "clinically dead" and CPR brought him back. He then overcame overwhelming odds to live. At the time we thought he was "over the hump" and going to make it, he tragically put his left eye out while still at the vet's. He developed septicemia from the injury and once more fought heroically for his life. Our vet stated he had never encountered a foal so determined to live. Bubby made it once again, and finally came home to us. His left eye was removed once he was strong enough to withstand the surgery.

He will remain with us at Havenbrook. His joyful exuberance toward life is truly worth more than any amount of money.

Bubby delights his visitors with some unique antics. If he feels he is not the center of attention, he will lightly paw at your shoes. This progresses to untying shoes (he is especially fond of Velcro). If still ignored, he promptly lies down at your feet and rolls over, "accidentally" bumping the offender. At this time if you scratch his belly he will bob his head up and down and flail his legs, looking much like a dog getting a tummy scratching. He is definitely one in a million, has his own magazine slot called "Bub's Corner," and is beloved by all who visit.

On October 23, 2000, Bubby began persistently running to our living room window, as the glass doors looked out on his paddock. He was loudly calling an alarm, and when we went to investigate his strange behavior, found the neighbor's 15-hand stallion had jumped our pasture fence and was savaging our mares and literally killing

"Encore," our herd stallion. Without Bub's prompt action and the intelligence to somehow know to try and get help for his friends, the outcome would have been much worse. We always knew he was special and he proved once more just what a tiny hero he is!

Havenbrooks Bubby.

A Dream Come True

By Joyce Salado
Highland Joy Farm
Grove City, Ohio

I was out in the barn cleaning and working with the minis when a friend came over. She didn't even stop at the house; she just knew I would be in the barn. She came to tell me about a pony near her that was being mistreated, and what we could do about it. She wanted some grain and hay to take to it since it looked starved. So we went right over there. No one was home, so we didn't have to ask to feed it. We found two small miniature horses, not ponies. Oh my, they were in terrible condition, no food or water, and standing knee-deep in manure. Both of them had cuts and flies all over them, you could hardly tell what color they were with all the dirt and manure all over them. They were frightened of us and moved to the other side of the tiny makeshift stall. We put in the hay and went to get buckets of water. My first thought was to call the authorities and report this, but I wanted to wait until the people came home. I was going to try to buy them and rescue them.

That evening I went back, and the people were home. The kids had one of the minis out on a rope, hitting it with a big stick. It was terrified. I ran over to the kids and grabbed the rope, and petted the poor mini. The kids called him Trigger. They were too big to ride him but they were getting on him anyway. A bigger boy threw a big rock and hit Trigger in the neck. Another kid ran up and almost pulled his tail off. That was it. I had to stop this. I talked to the people and offered to buy Trigger, and the other one. No deal. They wanted to keep them for the kids and grandkids. So I informed them that I would report what I had seen. They didn't know I had taken pictures when I was there earlier. They had already taken out the bucket of water. They were still beating on Trigger when I left, but they said they would feed them and clean out the shed.

When I went back the next morning, nothing had been done, so I cleaned, so they could at least feel better. A friend helped shovel out for hours and put in bedding. It was so hot in there. I just had a feeling, what should I do? I wanted to buy the animals before reporting it. One more try. One more attempt to get them. No one was home, and a neighbor said they went out of town for a few days. So, rescue mission was about to take place. I couldn't get home fast enough, to get the trailer to go back after them. I didn't feel like I was a horse thief. I backed up near the shed, ran in saying you're coming home, and a vet will be there. My heart was pounding, I hoped I was doing the right thing.

The authorities should have been called and these people punished, but then all the red tape you hear about. I still felt that I had to do something myself. I went in and the little one they called Rocky was lying down. I was too late. His suffering was over and he had already trotted over the Rainbow Bridge. I felt so bad. Through the tears I managed to get Trigger loaded. He was so terrified, he flinched and trembled all over. He had the biggest sad eyes. I went to the house and slid a note and a check under the door.

The vet arrived shortly after we got home. He said Trigger might not make it, but we had to try. I practically stayed with him all night. He was weak, but it was no time till he looked better to me. Something in his eyes said he'd be OK. The people never came after him. Never called or anything. I was worried that I'd be reported as a horse thief or something. I guess the letter I left them saying I would report it told them something. A neighbor reported it, the dead horse was still there. They were in trouble because of that and the filthy conditions, and got a fine, etc.

Slowly Trigger trusted me, and every day he was better. He was such a loving horse. Little guy was only 28" tall, a beautiful tri-color pinto. I heard later on that he had papers, but I didn't get them. He would do anything you asked. He followed me around like a puppy.

A little girl named Shelly comes every other week to visit the minis. Her mom drives nearly two hours to get here. Shelly was in a car accident when she was five years old and lost her right leg, and now she has her new prosthetic leg, and is doing so well. Horses were her dream. To ride and train horses. The past few years have been hard for Shelly and her family, but they always bring Shelly to visit the minis. There is nothing like the smile on her face.

She was excited to see Trigger for the first time. On her last visit, Trigger was still recovering and getting used to his new home, so I didn't have them meet. After a while with her favorite mini, a little mare named Candy, Shelly wanted to see Trigger. I told her he's a bit shy at first. I had already told her all about him, and she couldn't wait. Shelly is a little bit loud and excitable since the accident, so I thought Trigger would shy away from her. I was wrong. He went right up and nuzzled her. Friends at first sight.

They spent the afternoon together. Shelly brushed and brushed Trigger and he stood so still for everything she wanted to do. When Shelly had to go home, Trigger walked and walked the fence like he was looking for her.

Shelly came back in two weeks for her visit, but her parents let her be the one to tell me they were moving even farther away and she might not be able to come as often. Shelly was upset, but continued to brush and pet Trigger. Her mom asked if Shelly could have her tenth birthday party here at the farm and bring a couple of friends. Oh yes, we said, that would be a great idea, and we would be sure it was a lot of fun. A cookout was planned, a big cake decorated with a horse, lots of balloons and fun things to do. I bought Shelly a red bucket and filled it with her very own horse brushes and horse things.

The day of the party came, and several of her friends were able to come and some kids she had met here, and it was the best birthday party ever. Lots to eat, fun games, horses to pet. Then it was time for the presents. Everyone knew Shelly loved horses, so she got horse books and horse toys and a cowboy hat. She was delighted. I gave her the bucket full of brushes and things and she was so happy. She hugged and held on to the bucket. Her very own brushes! That smile couldn't get any bigger!

Then my daughter Monica came walking around the barn leading Trigger, in his new purple halter and lead rope. (Purple is Shelly's favorite color.) Trigger had a big purple bow around his neck. He walked all proud and bouncy up to Shelly, and she started brushing him with the new brushes. She said, "Now I have my very own brushes for you; you don't have to share with the other horses." Then Monica handed the purple lead rope to Shelly, and we all sang "Happy Birthday" and hugged Shelly. It was a few minutes before she realized Trigger was her birthday present. Everyone cried and smiled and laughed and sang. Shelly said, "That was my birthday wish, to have my very own horse!"

Now that Shelly's family had moved to a house with a couple of acres, they approved of my gift to Shelly. The two of them were meant to be together, both overcoming all odds against them, struggling to survive, and making each other so happy. That was two years ago, and they are still best friends. Trigger was trained to pull a cart, and takes Shelly every day. As much as I miss Shelly's visits and I miss Trigger, I know how happy they are. Her dream was to have a horse, and Trigger needed a little girl to love him. Shelly's accident was due to a drunk driver, and at times she nearly gave up the fight to live. After she came to visit the horses, she really perked up and looked forward to the visits. I'm so glad I rescued Trigger, and he was the perfect horse for Shelly. Everything worth working hard for has a happy ending. Shelly calls me and still visits once in awhile, but she is always anxious to get back to her very own horse, her dream come true.

A Lesson Learned

By Sharon K. Taylor
Mystic Rose Ranch
Jackson, California
www.horseminiature.net

It was during a small miniature horse show in a small Northern California town held in the heat of summer a few years back that a 16-year-old boy taught me an important lesson in sportsmanship.

I had asked Terry if he would show my stallion in the Youth Hunter class. He quickly agreed, for it was a class my stallion often won and I had high hopes for him again that day.

Terry was the first exhibitor to enter the ring and he skillfully ran through the course with my stallion; a clean run that to me seemed unbeatable. Together we stood and watched the next five horses either refuse a jump or knock at least one pole to the ground. Just one more competitor to beat and the blue ribbon would be ours.

However, the last to enter the ring was a young girl who, although new to competition, flawlessly circled the course with her gelding and it soon became apparent she would take the blue ribbon. But, then, just after easily clearing the last jump, she approached the gate where we were standing and appeared to forget to run through the required orange cones.

If she missed the cones, my stallion would be declared the winner and another blue ribbon would hang in my barn.

Then, to my surprise, Terry yelled out to her, "The cones. The cones," as I tried to hush him.

She quickly changed her direction in time to go through the cones and later, when the winner was named, the young girl walked up proudly to claim her first blue ribbon. My stallion and Terry would walk away with second place.

After leaving the ring, I said to Terry, "You know, if you hadn't reminded her of the cones, you would have won the blue ribbon."

A puzzled look came over Terry's face. "But she deserved to win," he said. "She had a better go." It was plain to me then that Terry wouldn't have wanted to win because of the young girl's disqualification. Winning wasn't the most important thing to him as it had been for me.

I walked away from the ring that day, disappointed. But I was disappointed, not for placing second. I was disappointed in myself. Several years have passed and I still remember the lesson learned at that small show, in that small town, in the heat of summer, when a 16-year-old boy taught me the spirit of sportsmanship.

Sharon's stallion making a jump.

After nearly a decade of involvement with miniature horses, each year I become even more convinced that this breed somehow attracts the best of our youth and brings out the best in each of them.

Two Miracles

By Kathy Atchley
Sunrise Hill Farm
Ponder, Texas
www.sunrisehillfarm.com

The Midnight Miracle

It was May, 1999. My sorrel pinto mare Criss Cross was due to foal, and I had had her up in the barn for weeks, watching her. She was a maiden mare and was bred to a champion pinto stallion, and I wasn't about to miss this baby. Her pregnancy had been normal, and on the evening of May 24, I could tell this would be the night. Criss Cross was restless and having diarrhea, and didn't eat all of her grain that day. Instead of going back in the house to watch her on the TV monitor, I decided to stay in the barn and sit with her, since she seemed comforted by my presence.

Around 11 p.m., Criss Cross went into labor, alternately lying down, getting up, and rolling. I got my rubber gloves, iodine and a towel ready. Finally her water broke, then the white bubble appeared under her wrapped tail, and then one little white hoof. Normal so far. Criss Cross strained and strained, and then a nose appeared, then more of the head. No other front leg! Time to put on the gloves and see what was going on. I very carefully felt around inside her for the missing right foreleg. I couldn't find it. I ran to the tack room phone and called my vet. Then I went to the house and got my husband Dale to help me. While Dr. Ingram was on his way, Dale held Criss Cross up and still, so I could try again to find the leg. By this time, the foal's entire head was hanging out. The sac had broken from around its face, but the foal hung there limply. Its eyes were rolled back, tongue hanging out, not responding. I was sure it was dead. It seemed like hours before the vet got there, but it was really only minutes. By this time Criss Cross had been straining and pushing for half an hour, with very little progress.

Sunrise Hill Farm Midnight Miracle.

When Dr. Ingram's truck pulled up to the barn, Dale and I were standing in the doorway. I said, the foal is dead. Dr. Ingram didn't say anything, just got his equipment and entered the foaling stall. Dale and I held Criss Cross up against the stall wall while Dr. Ingram's plastic-sleeved arm went inside her to try to find the right foreleg. It took him a long time to find it. The whole time, Criss Cross was straining, pushing, trying to lie down, and opening her mouth in an awful silent scream. Dale and I were trying to hold up and comfort a mare who wanted to go down, and all of us, including Criss Cross, were covered in sweat, hair and blood. It was hot and airless in the stall, and it seemed to take forever.

Finally Dr. Ingram found the other foreleg and got it up over the pelvis, and then the entire foal slid completely out with a plop onto the ground. It was motionless. It was a beautiful, tiny, sorrel pinto filly, and it appeared to be dead. While we stood there catching our breath, and while Criss Cross went down, panting and sweating in exhaustion, Dale said he thought he saw one of the filly's ears flicker slightly. Dr. Ingram immediately grabbed the baby by her hind legs and starting swinging her back and forth to clear her lungs of amniotic fluid. When he stopped and laid the foal back down, she lifted up her head and looked around as if to say, what's all the fuss about?

Since it was midnight and the filly was miraculously alive after this ordeal, we named her Sunrise Hill Midnight Miracle.

Although Miracle looked fairly normal at birth, it was obvious as time went on that she was not going to grow normally. Her head was too large, her legs too short, and she had an underbite. Our little Miracle was a dwarf. Fortunately, she has not had any health problems as so many other dwarf minis do. She is now over two years old and has measured 25" tall for over a year. She will never be bred or shown, but she is valuable in other ways. Her worth is measured in the joy she brings to others. Miracle is the farm favorite, has more visitors than any of the other horses, and has a busier social calendar than we, her owners, do. She has been in parades and petting zoos, attended children's birthday parties, gone to an elementary school for show and tell, and visited a nursing home to cheer up the residents. Her presence has been requested at numerous functions. No need to hook up the horse trailer for Miracle; she will hop right in the back seat and ride in your vehicle. She's been bathed in the bathtub, taken inside houses, and trots up stairs like an old pro. She has brought joy to numerous lives, and will live here until she dies. We're just grateful to have our little midnight miracle.

The 288-Day Miracle

August 15, 2001 was a typical hot, sunny day in Texas. I went out to feed about 8 a.m. as usual, and fed all the minis on my property before going to feed the mares next door, in the three-acre pasture we lease from our neighbors. I poured the grain into each feeder and counted heads to make sure all the horses were accounted for. One short. Southern Belle was not there. I scanned the pasture but did not see her. My heart plummeted; I knew something was wrong. Belle was always first in line waiting to eat.

I had gotten Belle the previous October, a beautiful two-year-old, open, bay pintaloosa mare. I normally would not have put her with a stallion until early spring, but she was so unexpectedly hard to catch and handle, I was afraid if I turned her loose in one of the large pastures, I'd never see her again. So I decided to keep her in the small pasture next to the barn, with my appaloosa stallion, so I could see and handle her more often. I put her there on November 1, and figured she'd come into heat in February or March. On December 1, I did my annual mid-winter ultrasound rechecks to make sure everyone who was bred earlier in the year was still bred. To my surprise, Southern Belle sonogrammed 30 days pregnant. She was more trusting of me by that time, and easier to handle, so I moved her over to the leased pasture so that she could be with other bred mares.

Since I ultrasound often, and my vet is very accurate, I usually know almost to the day when my mares conceived, and I keep a calendar and chart of each mare's gestation and make a note of each subsequent ultrasound recheck to confirm the dates. When each mare reaches the 300-day gestation mark (when foals are generally considered to be viable), I put her up in the barn in a comfortable, monitored stall, and start watching. Even if Southern Belle had conceived on November 1, the very day I put her with my stallion, she would be only 288 days along on August 15. (She had never been with a stallion before that date.) I had not planned to stall her for another two weeks, and a quick examination of her just a couple of days ago had not shown any signs at all of imminent foaling.

All this was going through my head as I hurried back to the barn to get a halter and lead rope. Then I went back to the leased pasture and went looking for Belle. I felt in my heart that she had already foaled, too early, and I would find a dead baby. We'd already lost three foals this foaling season and I would be heartbroken to have another death.

I found Belle on the other side of the large shelter, standing over a small blob. When I got closer I saw that the blob was a foal, and it was alive and attempting to stand up. Its legs were too wobbly and crooked, and it was the tiniest foal I had ever seen.

Belle tried to kick me when I got closer, so I moved slowly and talked to her gently, and she finally let me pick up the foal. It was a solid gray colt. He weighed almost nothing. I started to make the long walk back to my barn, with the baby in my arms and Belle circling around me whinnying. I stopped only when I saw the placenta on the ground, just long enough to check that it was all there and complete. When I got up to the gate, Belle wouldn't let me catch her, she was way too upset, even to come with me and her foal. I left her in the pasture and took the baby into the barn. I measured him at just under 15" tall. He was not a dwarf; he was perfectly conformed, except for the rubbery legs.

After I settled him in a clean stall, I went back for Belle. It took about half an hour to catch her but I finally did, and put her in the stall with her baby. She settled down almost immediately, but was still overprotective enough that she would try to kick me every time I went into the stall. For a maiden mare, she certainly knew that this was her baby, and she wanted him all to herself!

Sunrise Hill Farm Silver Lining.

The foal was so weak, and Belle didn't have much of a bag, so I called my vet immediately. Dr. Ingram came over right away to examine the premature foal. He gave him a tetanus shot, we iodined his navel and did all the usual things you do to a newborn. By the time the vet left, the foal was standing better but was still too unbalanced to nurse. I spent most of the day milking out the mare, forcing her to produce more, and feeding him with a bottle.

By afternoon, the foal seemed weaker, even though I had barely left the barn, and was feeding him as much as I could. Back came Dr. Ingram, and tubed the foal with colostrum. I kept watch for the rest of the day and night, and most of the next few days. Finally the colt could stand long enough to nurse by himself, and his mom had an adequate bag by that time. Every day the colt's weak, wobbly legs would be a little stronger. Dr. Ingram checked his medical records and confirmed that this was a 288-day foal, and was amazed not only that he was alive, but that he had no serious health problems. He kept warning me not to get too attached or name him yet; he said he wasn't out of the woods yet.

After about a week, when it was more evident that the colt was going to make it, I asked the vet, "Is it OK to name him yet?" And he said yes. I knew then the little guy was truly out of danger. My friend Sue High came over to see him, and suggested the name Sunrise Hill Farm Silver Lining. It seemed to fit him. He truly is a silver lining in what could have been a very dark cloud. Silver Lining is still barely 17" tall at two months old, and he still wobbles when he walks and falls occasionally, but is a healthy and active colt, one that everyone who visits the farm falls in love with!

Postscript: A sad ending to this story. On November 5 we found Silver Lining dead in his stall with his mom standing over him. He had appeared healthy up until this point. His sudden and unexpected death was a shock to us, but we have to assume it was due in some way to his prematurity. We are grateful for the short time he was with us, and he will be greatly missed.

The Haligonian Farm Story

By Harriett Rubins
Haligonian Farm
Canandaigua, New York
www.haligonianfarm.com

Our First Mare

In 1988 I had no minis whatsoever. I was determined to get some, having sold my thoroughbred racehorses which were wearing me down and making me grow old fast. I figured after getting my 1,200-pound racehorses ready for the track a little mini would be a piece of cake. How much trouble could they be? If they didn't behave, I figured I'd just pick 'em up and put 'em where they needed to be. So I started looking for one.

The very first place I went was to a horse dealer who had an advertisement in the local paper. It was just what I thought I needed, a black and white pinto mare. I called, made the appointment and went to look. It was love at first sight. Tied to a fence in his yard was a shining black and white "Oreo cookie," black on both front and back ends, white in the middle. She had a long, flowing mane and tail and great big doleful eyes. He said her name was "Justa Smidge." Very fitting name, I thought. I had to have her. We dickered for awhile and came to an agreement on her price. I gave him a deposit, promising to pay the balance when he brought the mare. After working out the details for the delivery, I left to get ready for her arrival.

The day didn't come too soon. I was so excited as the dealer drove in with his 30+ foot gooseneck rig attached to his dually, with my one little mini inside. Not even turning off the truck, he handed me the end of Smidge's lead rope, held out his hand for his money, put an envelope with what I assumed to be Smidge's papers in my other hand, said,

"Good Luck," hopped back in his truck and backed down our long driveway like a freight train.

I looked at Smidge. She looked at me and we headed for the barn. We spent the day together. I brushed her, picked her hooves, walked her down the road to show all the neighbors, strolled on a path in the woods, followed the electric fence line so she'd know her boundaries and did what I thought was "bonding." I told her how I already loved her and we were going to be buddies.

That night I took out her papers to get the transfer signed and sent in with me as Smidge's owner. Her registration paper didn't read "Justa Smidge." It said her name was "Gone Again." Uh oh, I thought, what a strange name.

The next day I had to go in to work. I was a teacher at that time. I turned Smidge out in her own paddock next to the pasture with my riding horses and left. She was contentedly munching grass. When I came home, I couldn't find her. She had lived up to her name. She was gone. I searched everywhere, called the neighbors, and called the sheriff's department. Nothing. No one had seen her. I was frantic, but there was nothing more I could do except wait until she was spotted. I walked the fence line to try to see where she had gotten out. There were no breaks in the wire.

Smidge.

About 6 p.m., tears in my eyes, I went out and rattled the feed bucket, calling the riding horses in for dinner. They ambled to the barn door and I led them to their stalls. It couldn't have been more than a minute or two and there was Smidge trotting through the door, nickering for her dinner. I'm sure she had a smile on her face. Needless to say, I was overjoyed.

For days after that, but only on weekdays when I had to go to school, Smidge would disappear, only to reappear for evening feed. One day, I think it was a school holiday when I was home but she thought I'd be away, I spied on her. She carefully got down on her belly and easily slid under the electric wire. Then she sauntered into the woods. I followed at a distance and found her in another pasture calmly grazing alongside a small black pony. Evidently, she figured this gelding was more her size, or maybe she thought he was lonely. Whatever it was, they were buddies. I bought the pony, which turned out to be a "B" sized mini, and brought him home. And then there were two.

Smidge stayed home once Sparkles was on the property. Eventually, when I registered her, I changed her name to Justa Smidge. (You could do that in the old days before the registry was closed.)

Our First Stallion

My first stallion, bought in 1989, was Rudolf van Double Dutch, a 30" black and white stallion imported from Holland. He was a stocky little fellow and quite opinionated as most working stallions can be. But he was also a gentleman—kind and gentle. When he was out in pasture, I could call to him and he'd round up his mares and bring them up to the gate to say hello and get some treats.

It's very cold in the Finger Lakes of western New York. So, in the winter the horses go out during the day as the weather permits, but they're in the barn at night.

One evening, after the horses were in the barn, a neighbor and her eight-year-old son came for a quick visit. The mom and I got to talking and the boy got restless. To give us more time to chat, I took a brush, handed it to the youngster and told him he could pick out a horse, go in its stall and groom it.

The neighbor and I continued our chat, totally forgetting about the boy. I don't know how much time had passed when we heard the screech, "Ma…!" from one of the stalls.

"Oh my God," I cried out. "He's in the stallion's stall." I ran toward the howl, thinking that the stallion had injured the boy.

When I got to the stall, there was the little fellow sitting on the floor of the stall with Rudy lying next to him, his head in the child's lap. The boy had sat down cross-legged under the stallion and was brushing Rudy's belly. The stallion loved the attention. I'm sure he figured out that a better way to get a larger area brushed was to present a big target for the small hand—so he stretched out next to his new friend.

Rudy.

We knew Rudy was a nice stallion, but it was at that point we realized how wonderful and invaluable this little stallion is. At that time I was an elementary school teacher. I could take Rudy from his pasture full of mares, doll him up with a bath and braids and take him into school, to be mauled by 350 kids. He never once had an accident in school. In fact, I had to put him in the trailer to relieve himself. He didn't even want to mess up the lawn outside the school, although he was willing to mow it.

Rudolf van Double Dutch is 21 now. Justa Smidge is 22. They are still here at Haligonian Farm, living out their lives in retirement.

And that was our start. Now there are usually around 50 minis here at Haligonian Farm. And I love every one.

Billy and the Tank

By Fran Curtis
Lucky C Farm Miniature Horses
Justin, Texas
facurtis@hotmail.com

Years ago, long before we became seriously interested in minis, we owned a few of them. Our two youngest daughters were small, and although we owned several large Quarter Horses, we thought the minis would be great on which Casey and Ashley could learn haltering and grooming. Thus we acquired Blue and Tank. True to his name, Tank was very short, very broad, and very sturdy. He was also very mellow. The girls also had several pygmy goats at this time.

Not being familiar with minis, we were afraid to put them out with the big horses, so we pastured them with the goats. The billy goat, appropriately named "Billy," wasn't much smaller than Tank and was considerably cantankerous. It soon became Billy's favorite thing to stand beside Tank and proceed to bring his horns up under Tank's belly or gently butt him in the side. We were constantly chastising Billy and chasing him away, but as soon as we left, he would return to his favorite game of "butt the tank." We didn't worry too much as it was obvious Tank wasn't being harmed.

One day I was working with a young horse in an adjoining paddock when I noticed Billy harassing Tank. I stopped what I was doing and started walking over to chase Billy away. Apparently, however, that was the very day that Tank had had enough. I was just a few feet from the gate when it happened. Billy was butting Tank in the side, as usual. Tank spun around, chomped down on Billy's neck, planted his hindquarters and began to spin around. It only took one full revolution for Billy's feet to be straight out, parallel to the ground. Tank's "sit and spin" made some of my Quarter Horses look bad. They weren't that good with training!

After about six revolutions, Tank let go. Billy flew a short distance, landing head over heels. Totally uninjured but massively dizzy, Billy staggered around for several minutes just trying to stay upright. Tank had already forgotten the entire thing and was off grazing.

We owned Billy and Tank for a long time after that day. Billy found a new game to play, called "tear down all fences," and although he and Tank never did become friends, Billy never bothered Tank again.

A Memorable Horse Sale

By Ken and Betty Grieger
Cedar Drive Farm
Elizabethtown, Indiana
www.cedardrivefarm.com

My wife and I have been raising miniature horses for several years. During this time we have sold a good many horses to people in several states and overseas. There was one sale that has been quite memorable. This involves a gentlemen by the name of Benny and his wife Wilma.

Benny and Wilma visited one day and wanted to look at some of our miniatures. Benny walked with the aid of a cane and during the course of introductions and further conversation Benny stated he was 80 years old and had a heart condition. My initial thought was why would he want some miniature horses.

As we showed them some of the miniatures it became obvious that Benny was going to buy some horses. He had no interest in pinto horses and finally settled on a couple of dun fillies.

I delivered the horses a few days later. In the process of finding Benny's farm I had to stop and ask directions. The lady I talked to exclaimed, "You must have Benny's minis." Apparently Benny had spread the word that he was getting some little horses

During the course of the next few months the following things happened in a rather fast fashion:

Benny stopped by one day to show me a set of harness he purchased for the horses. It was a really nice harness and Benny was very proud of what he had. I visited Benny a short time later and he showed me a wagon he had purchased. All cleaned up and freshly painted.

The next time Benny visited, he got out of his truck and was walking without the aid of his cane. Wilma stated that the horses made him get out of his easy chair and he was much more active.

Benny and Wilma stopped by one time after Benny had been to the doctor. Wilma said the doctor was pleasantly surprised at the progress Benny was making. Again it was a result of the horses and the care they needed that forced Benny to get around.

During a later visit, Benny showed me a photo of his horses hitched to the wagon. With the help of his son he had the horses broke as a team.

During the above time it is hard to describe the look in Benny's eyes. In brief he was very happy and very proud of what he had accomplished with the horses. At his age one can see why he felt the way he did.

Seeing the joy these horses provided this gentleman is why this was a very memorable sale.

The Christmas "Mini" Miracle

'Twas the night before Christmas,
The aroma ran deep,
Of apples, molasses, and
Hot mashes steeped.

Tiny hooves pawed
In contented delight,
At this special-made dinner
On Christmas Eve night.

The "Lady" had pet
And kissed each velvet nose,
Then wiped off their chins
Where the icicles froze.

With their bellies all full
From their holiday treat,
They all settled down
For a long winter's sleep.

The minis all snuggled
In their deep bedded stalls,
With their long winter coats
Looked like tiny fur-balls.

A new snow was falling
To blanket the ground,
Outside of the barn
And the "sleepers" so sound….

Sound…but for one
Little mare on the end,
Recovering from flu
Was put there to mend.

She awoke with a pain
That would not go away,
Then rolled and broke out
In a sweat where she lay.

She rolled and she groaned
And she kicked out in pain
But all her attempts
At relief were in vain.

She finally gave up and just
Lay on her side,
Too exhausted to move
She felt like she'd died.

The others were all waking up
From this din,
And craning their necks
In the direction 'twas in.

They instinctively knew
That their friend was in trouble,
And needed to get her
Some help on the double!

They all started stomping,
And kicking and neighing,
"Maybe, the Lady will hear us
And know what we are saying!"

But…nobody came,
Despite all their trying,
And each worried alone
That their friend may be dying.

When mysteriously
All the stall doors swung wide,
And turned them all loose
To be by her side.

As they all crowded 'round
And gazed in her stall,
She seemed to pull strength
From her friends at the wall.

This time she pushed hard!
With all her might.
She knew that she must,
She knew it was right.

The night held its breath
On this magical morn,
As on-looking friends
"Willed" her foal to be born.

He lay there so quiet,
Alongside the mare
No breathing…no motion
As still as the air.

She breathed loving whispers
Of life in his nose,
As the herd watched in awe
As his little chest rose.

The mare nuzzled her baby
With motherly love,
Then with a low nicker
She looked up above…

At her stablemates' faces
Surrounding her stall
And in her own way,
With her eyes, thanked them all.

She tenderly licked the wet
From her son,
To stop him from shaking,
And when she was done…

She nudged him so gently
To get him to stand
Back legs…then front…
Oh, he looked so grand!

The herd bowed their heads
In his presence to say,
That he was the "Prince"
On this Christmas Day.

A new star shone down
On the stable that night,
Where the minis all gathered
To help their friend's plight.

If you are a "doubter"
I tell you, it's true!
It all happened exactly
The way I've told you.

And…magic can happen…
And "Princes" are born…
Especially in stables…
On Christmas morn.

By Dona Neargarder
Kickapoo Acres, Fletcher, Ohio
http://kickapoo-acres.virtualave.net

Last Chance Prizefighter aka "Rocky"

By Mona Stone
Last Chance Miniatures
Sleeman, Ontario
http://www.jam21.net/lcminis

Our brave little colt that we named after the fighter "Rocky" because of his strong will to survive, and to overcome each hurdle as they came his way, and do so like he was a perfectly normal foal! Here is "Rocky's Story"…

This is our story about one special little horse named "Rocky." Rocky was born on April 11, 1999. He had a rough start right from the get-go…he was born in a mud puddle! I had his dam in the barn under camera for weeks, and finally, it was such a beautiful spring day, I decided to let her out into the round pen for some fresh air and sunshine; after all, she showed no signs of imminent foaling. I left her stall door open, as well as the barn door and the gate from the barn to the round pen. That way, if she did decide to do something, she could at least get back into her nice dry stall.

My daughter and I were sitting at the table playing cribbage when on the monitor, we could hear "Lyndsey" (Rocky's dam) running in and out, and in and out of the barn. That was not like her, so I jumped up and looked out the patio door to see a small body thrashing around out there!

I rushed out there, to find a little black body gasping and choking for air, covered in mud and lying in a mud puddle. I immediately scooped him up, and brought him into the barn, where I began drying him off with straw. I hollered at my daughter to bring some towels out to help clean and dry him off. When she got back out to the barn with the towels, I asked her to rub him down while I went to call the vet. I figured he must have inhaled a good portion of water and feared pneumonia. The vet said to give him $\frac{1}{2}$ cc of long-lasting penicillin then, and again the next day.

The colt was not coming around as he should, so I took his temperature to find it had dropped to below the hypothermia level. It was important to get his body temp back up, and fast! My husband brought some warm water-filled garbage bags, which we used to lay Rocky on to help raise his temp. I was using an electric hair dryer to blow warm air all over his body, as well as to dry him off. He was now starting to show his pretty buckskin pinto colorings, and was also showing his will to survive. Lyndsey stood back patiently and watched, seeming to know that we were there for no other reason than to help her new son. He was very weak, but continually showed signs of improvement, and he would bounce from side to side, and all around, just when trying to hold his own head up. It was sad to see, and I thought for sure we would lose him.

Rocky.

After we got him as dry and as warm as possible, it was time for him to nurse. We were not able to, so gave him his colostrum by syringe, and then I would go out and milk his dam and feed him by syringe every couple of hours. I was not able to get him to actually nurse until the next day. He would nuzzle and mouth his dam, but would not actually latch onto her. It was such a great sight when he finally did!

Rocky was born with an extremely undershot mouth, and very bad legs. I was not real worried about the mouth, as I figured it should straighten out on its own in time. It was his legs that had me worried. His front ones were bad, but nowhere near as bad as his back legs! On his right rear, it looked as though the ankle was set on crooked and that the tendon ran a diagonal line from his hock to his fetlock joint. He had very lax tendons, and when he stood, was not up on his hooves at all, and you could actually see the bottoms of his hooves as they faced forward, just as a person's feet are out in front of their ankle. It was a sorry sight, but Rocky didn't seem to mind!

I took him to the vet, and Dr. Cannon did x-rays to see just what was going on in there. What had happened was that the outside edge of the cannon bone was growing faster than the inside edge and that was causing the bad twist to the ankle joint. He splinted and wrapped the one (right) hind leg and left the other alone, as it was not as bad. I was to return in one week for reassessment. After the first week, and as soon as he removed the splint, there was a noticeable improvement, so he re-wrapped the leg, and did the other one also this time. It only lasted a couple of days, and it started to fall off the leg, becoming more of a hindrance than a help. I cut it off, and brought him back again to have it redone.

After two more weeks in this wrap, it was clear to see that it was doing him no good at all. There was no ankle support, and his feet were still buckled under his legs from the very lax tendons. He and his dam had been on pretty much complete stall rest, as we had a lot of rainy weather, and he was not allowed to get it wet, as this could cause the leg underneath to rot. The wraps were removed and we were now faced with a decision to make. Rocky could clearly not live like this because he would wear the hide and meat to the bone. He needed his hooves to walk on. Would we have to make the decision to put him to sleep?

After discussing this with my vet, he also agreed that Rocky could not live like that, but it seemed such a shame to have to put him to sleep. He said that Rocky was so easy to work with, we would have to try one more thing first. On May 20th, Rocky got brand new fiberglass casts on each of his hind legs. If this works, we will work on the front legs (which aren't as severe) after the hind legs have been fixed.

He is now able to go outside and play as long as it is not wet out. The fiberglass casts are waterproof, but the cotton tube and gauze wrap sticks out the bottom of the cast a little, and would work as a wick to draw the moisture up inside of the cast, and that is not good, as it could possibly cause the skin inside the cast to rot.

Rocky will now wear his casts until June 3, when I will take him back to have the casts removed for an evaluation. If there is even the slightest improvement, we will continue with the casts, but if not, unfortunately, we will have tried all we can, and will have to face the fact that he must be put to sleep so as to not have him suffer throughout life for our selfishness.

June 3, 1999 update—We took Rocky to the vet today for his cast removal and evaluation, and we are sorry to say it was not good news. There was no improvement at all. I decided to hold off putting him to sleep until I try just one more thing. A person wrote to me and told me about a product that she thought may help. It is called Hoof Pro. Dr. Cannon gave his honest opinion that he doesn't think it will do any good at all, but I want to at least give it a try. I will see if I can find this product and begin Rocky on it ASAP. He is now in splints again, just to give him some ankle support and to keep him up on his hooves. Wish us luck, for this is Rocky's last hope!

We feel that even though Rocky was not real small at birth, he is a dwarf. He has several dwarf characteristics which include an undershot jaw, short neck, poor legs, and chunky body, and since we have never had a dwarf before, we feel that Rocky must be our first! What he lacks in conformation, he surely makes up in character! He is truly one special little man!

June 15, 1999 update—I finally received the Hoof Pro powder that I had been waiting for that Joanne was sending me. I haven't even given him any yet, as I am waiting for usage directions, but I already know in my heart that we will have to put him to sleep. Tonight when I went out to put Rocky and his mom into the barn for the night, I decided to take off the splint, as he seemed to be limping on it. (He still has the cast on the other leg.) When I removed the splint, I found a sore on his leg where the splint had been rubbing. It is not a bad sore, but it should be given the time to air out and heal. It looks so painful for him to walk on. It never seemed to bother him in the past, but now he is showing definite signs of pain. I don't know if I will be able to watch the poor little guy stumble around in pain for the next few weeks while waiting for the powder to do its magic, and then finding out it has done nothing but prolong his agony. I am really unsure as to which way to turn. I think I will try to give him a chance with this powder, but if the pain seems to get to be too much for him, I will choose to put him to sleep even if his few weeks aren't up yet. He basically is walking on the bottom end of his cannon bone, and the full underside of the hoof can be seen while looking straight on.

June 22, 1999 update—We took Rocky to the vet today to have his other cast removed, as he has been favoring that leg over the weekend, so I figured he must have a sore under there. When we got there, I asked my vet to see if he could get some approximate prices for me as to what it would cost for surgery. He said, "For an orthopedic surgeon to do surgery, you are looking at no less than $1000 per leg, and that's probably a LOW estimate." I broke down then, as I knew that Rocky would need two, and possibly three legs done, and we just didn't have that kind of money for the surgery, and no guarantee it would even be beneficial.

We took him in and removed his cast. As soon as we were able to get it off, you could see the stuff that had drained onto the gauze from his sore, and the smell was putrid! We got the gauze wrap off, and there was a big gaping hole (similar to that of a donut hole) in his leg. We put him on the ground and it was instantly obvious that we would not let Rocky go on this way.

We made arrangements to have the vet come out and put Rocky to sleep for us tomorrow, but then realized that it will be our daughter's graduation, and just too busy a day for it, so we rescheduled for Thursday. It was such a hard decision, but our vet, my husband and myself, all knew it was time, and we all wanted to do what was best for our little Rocky. Where he was just a little uncomfortable before with his casts, and less agile than the other foals, he was now clearly showing signs of pain, and there would be none of that where I was concerned. I knew we had done everything that we could for him, and his time had come. We made the decision to do it at home, with his mom and in their stall. This way, his mom would know (sense) that he had died, and her parting with him would not be so difficult, thus making it easier on her too.

June 24, 1999 update—Well, this was really a hard morning for us. I let Rocky and his mom out of the stall and into the round pen just off of the barn. It was a beautiful bright sunny morning, which helped to make the day less dreary. It was a beautiful day for Rocky for his last day on earth.

We spent all morning with him, cuddling and talking to him, and saying our good-byes before the vet came. We decided to do "it" right where he was lying in the bright sunshine, instead of bringing him into the barn. We left his mom with him for an hour afterwards, before my husband took him to bury him. It will be easier for his mom too now, as she now knows he is "gone."

Rocky will suffer no more, and all of his days will be just as they were today…bright and sunny, but without pain.

"Rest in peace, little man"…you have really touched our lives, and we will miss you, but we will meet up with you again, some day. Thank you, for being so special.

My Hero

By Nona Lacy
Little Lacy's Miniature Horse Farm
McLouth, Kansas

Often times when someone finds out that I own miniature horses, they ask, "What are they good for?" I am sure this is a question that you have had the pleasure of answering as well. You and I know that there are a lot of things they are good for. Showing, driving, teaching children about horses, taking them to nursing homes are just a few of things you might mention. However, now I have a new story to tell when someone asks me, "What are they good for?"

My good friend, Sandy of Serenity Acres Miniature Horse Farm, had planned to attend a two-day seminar on photography with her husband. Sandy had two mares that were within a couple of weeks of foaling and we all know that they can be unpredictable at times and deliver when we least expect it. I volunteered to go check on the mares every so often throughout both days, just to make sure we had no newcomers to the farm without proper supervision.

I made my way over in the morning of the first day. My husband had an appointment so he dropped my two kids and me off at Serenity Acres and left. The three of us proceeded to feed the horses and then we returned to the foaling stalls where I busied myself by doting over the expectant mothers. Having a horse farm ourselves, I knew my kids were pretty horse-savvy, but four-year-olds can be as unpredictable as, well to put it mildly, tornadoes. (And if you know Crystal, you will agree.) My son was quietly tucked away in the hay stall, playing his Game Boy, and Crystal, my four-year-old daughter, was doing her best to catch a kitty.

I turned around to put up a brush I had been using, and in those brief few seconds, Crystal went missing. It didn't take me long to figure out that she had disappeared into one of the last places I would want her to go alone. She had slipped through Silver Dollar's stall door, Sandy's stallion. Now, I knew rationally that Silver Dollar was for the most part a docile, calm, sweet little horse; however, he is still a stallion and I knew that a four-year-old had no business alone with any stallion.

Stuffy and Crystal.

As I headed for the stall I heard a soft nicker of warning from one of Sandy's other horses. It was Stuffy. Stuffy is a barren mare that Sandy had placed in Silver Dollar's paddock as company for the off-season stallion. When I got over to the stall, what I saw surprised me and gave me a new appreciation for our little friends. Crystal was standing inside the stall and Silver Dollar was at the door that leads to the paddock, and in between was Stuffy, sideways, keeping one eye on Crystal and one eye on Silver Dollar. She was determined to protect that little creature, which I am convinced she thought was some kind of weird-looking foal, from this big bad stallion.

I quickly removed Crystal from the stall and gave her the "Never go into any stalls without me!" talk, and then praised Stuffy for her brave act of heroism. Crystal says, "Stuffy saved me." I would have to agree, and if anyone asks me, "What are they good for?" I will say, "They may just be your hero" (or as far as Crystal is concerned, a new best friend).

How Sam Got His Name

By Sandy Martin
Serenity Acres Miniature Horse Farm
Leavenworth, Kansas
http://serenityacre.com

The month of April was filled with fear and promise, a typical beginning to foaling season at Serenity Acres Miniature Horse Farm in northeastern Kansas. Two experienced mares were due to foal. Adjustments were made to the primary barn—partitions taken down between stalls to turn four stalls into two large foaling stalls, camera cables were re-strung between the barn and the house, the closed-circuit monitors were adjusted and fresh batteries were put into the Birth Alert halter transmitters.

The mares each complied and delivered a filly and a stud colt, both sired by Lil' Nips Silver Dollar and both with nearly identical pinto markings. Textbook. Just like previous years. Early May was when the law of averages caught up with us with a vengeance. It was easy to dismiss the fact that a mare had aborted a filly at the 9th month, hers was no longer in the count. And another mare had been sold in her 10th month, so…discounting them, there were only three more foals due. Two were due in May to small, maiden mares and one in July to our favorite mare. These three foals were to be the get of Lucky Four Apaches Adonis and were eagerly awaited.

But…the morning of the 3rd of May began badly and went downhill from there. The foal due in July aborted but wouldn't pass through the birth canal. The vet was struggling to get it turned when one of the maiden mares went into labor in the next stall. It became apparent that she was in trouble when her foal didn't progress after the first five minutes, and at that point both mares were loaded into the trailer to be rushed to the clinic, some fifteen miles away. Two long-awaited fillies were lost that day, but the team of three vets and an assistant were able to save the lives of the mares. A mixed bag of blessings.

Sandy's grandson Ian Reiff with SAM.

How quickly things change! Now there was suddenly only one mare due, Shirley, and she was the other under 30" maiden mare. When her labor began two nights later I was right out there, crying and pleading as I tried to find a front leg that wasn't presenting. My vet had told me earlier that week to trust my experience and if a mare was in trouble to put her right into the trailer and get her to the clinic, that he'd meet me there as quickly as he could. That's what I did after I'd called him and my friend, Nona. He tried to return my call but wasn't able to get a connection. I'd been using the portable house phone in the barn and unthinkingly took it with me!

The first thing we saw when we led the mare into the clinic was a dead miniature foal on the floor mat. I felt badly for someone's loss, worried about my own mare and knew that the vet had not had a good week either! He went into immediate action with Shirley. He sedated her, then struggled, lying flat out on the floor, to push the foal's head and the leg that had been born back into the birth canal so that he could retrieve the lost leg. It wasn't easy; the mare had been straining for about 40 minutes by that time and the foal's head had begun to swell. No signs of life, but Doc kept working, dripping wet from sweat, amniotic fluid and blood. Suddenly there was a "pop" and the head went back in. In a wink he reached way into the mare and pulled both legs forward, then the head and the chest were born. Everyone was holding his or her collective breath, and so was the foal. But Doc wasn't going to lose this one! It took three well-placed, well-timed slaps with the back of his hand on the foal's rib cage before he was able to get that little heart jump-started. The foal took its first breath, raised its head and looked at Doc as if to say, "What'd ya' do that for?"

Well, this little guy was obviously special. He'd been born under very difficult circumstances but was perfect in every way. The next step was to give him a name. Nona had been present, as friend and student throughout this difficult week, so why not ask her to name this special little colt? Because of what we'd been through, and because he'd had such a near miss, she decided that he is "Serenity Acres Shurly A Miracle," or SAM for short!

Patriot's Day Parade

By Nona Lacy
Little Lacy's Miniature Horse Farm
McLouth, Kansas

It was a nice day for a parade, unlike the continuous rain that we had experienced for the last few days. It was a sunny Saturday in April. I had promised a pack of Cub Scouts two miniature horses to follow their float in the McLouth, Kansas, Patriot's Day Parade. I also promised several bales of straw as seats for the float. We got up early and had planned to take the straw down several hours before the parade so they could be placed on the float. Only having one vehicle, my husband would then return to hook up the trailer, we'd load up the horses and head for the parade lineup. I had spent the rainy days making one blanket of red, white and blue for our mare to wear and planning the outfit for our other colt to wear.

As I went out to feed that morning, I noticed the ground was still rather wet from our downpour, but seemed solid enough out by the barn. My husband decided to pull the car up to the barn to load the straw. Halfway there, the car got stuck. We started trying to get it out. We laid down boards, put down sand. We tried everything we could think of. After 45 minutes the car was still stuck and we were running out of time. We called our neighbors who had tractors in hopes that someone could come pull us out, but no one was home. We broke down and called a tow truck. Within 20 minutes he was there and began his pulling. Within ten minutes he had dug a hole halfway to the other side of the world and was himself, stuck. I couldn't believe it. Our day was quickly unraveling like a cheap rug!

It was now time to line up for the parade and we didn't even have the bales down to the float, not to mention two little horses. I called on a friend who lives nearby, only to find that she was not home. Fortunately, technology was on our side and her husband was able to reach her by cell phone. She was in town about 20 miles away, but was heading straight for our place. By this time the tow truck got himself unstuck and our car, but said no way when I asked him to pull our trailer to a solid place to hook up. My friend arrived in her Suburban, but still we had no trailer. A decision had to be made. The parade would start in 30 minutes. Finally an idea popped into my head. One horse would be better than nothing. I ran to the barn and got SAM, our 25" yearling colt. I had my husband grab our St. Bernard's dog kennel and we coaxed SAM to back in. We lifted him into the back of the Suburban and off we went. We arrived just in time. Everyone was lined up and the entry was blocked, but they cleared the way happily when we explained we had a horse in the back we had to get through. One man didn't look convinced, that is until SAM let out the biggest whinny I have ever heard. We threw a Tiger Cub shirt on SAM and he was the hit of the parade.

When everything was over, we put him back in the kennel and into the Suburban, and hit the road. Try that with a 15-hand horse! The Miniature Horse proves once again that worth doesn't always come in big sizes. In fact, smaller was definitely better!

Nona and SAM in the parade.

My Darling Buttercup

By Nancy Houghton
Woodstock North Minis
Nevis, Minnesota
http://customer.unitelc.com/woodstockminis/

She was my heart. Buttercup was the first mini horse that we ever bought. She was exactly 38" tall and was a sorrel appaloosa with a marvelous white mane and tail that was like cotton candy, and I called her Sister Goldenhair. She had a gorgeous floating trot that could take your breath away. I taught her to shake hands, and tell me how old she was by pawing, but she could never get past eight years old, even thought I had her for 12 years.

January 9th loomed as a cold, miserable day in Northern Minnesota, with the temperature 20 degrees below zero. I went out to do the usual morning chores, and there was Buttercup lying down, rolling and sweating. Panic overcame me, and I immediately called the vet. He came right out and tubed her with mineral oil and gave her Banamine, and we figured that she was going to be all right.

My husband was in bed desperately sick with the flu, so he could not help me walk her. I walked her as long as I could with my heart condition, and as the afternoon progressed, she was not getting better and continued to roll every time I stopped walking her. The vet came again and tubed her again and gave her more Banamine, but she was still not better. He told me to call a specialist that was three hours away. I called and talked to him and he told me the treatment was correct and to keep on walking her. So I was at the exhausted point by now and totally freezing to death, so I called some dear friends of mine, Carmen and Joline Skogstad, and they drove two hours in the cold to come and help me walk her. We took turns walking her for most of the night in 25-degree-below-zero temps.

We were in touch by phone with the specialist, and he told us if she was not better by morning to drive her in. At 8 a.m. she was not better, so we started the three-hour drive to the specialist. We got her to the specialist, and he gave her more Banamine and tubed her again and told us that we had to leave her there so we went home to get some rest.

The next morning the vet called and said there was no improvement, and that she would have to have immediate colic surgery, and that the bill for the surgery would be $4500. We of course did not have this kind of money, so I made the decision to have her put down. But my husband, knowing how much I loved her, called the vet and told him to go ahead with the surgery anyhow, and that we would find the money somehow to pay for it. The vet did the surgery, called us and said that she had come through it fine, and was going to be OK. And we were so relieved that she was going to be okay, and made plans to go see her the next day.

Buttercup.

The next morning we went out to feed the horses and came in to find a message on the answering machine to call the vet right away. He told us that our darling Buttercup was dead, that she was in severe distress/pain and he had to put her down, and didn't even ask our permission first. The shock was almost more than we could handle, and I remember screaming and screaming and couldn't stop screaming for what seemed like hours. The pain was so intense I thought it would tear my heart out of my body to know that I would never see her in the pasture again or to call her my darling Buttercup again.

Her empty stall screamed to me for a year after we lost her and I came very close to having a nervous breakdown after losing her; and it has been two years now, and the pain is as fresh as if it were yesterday.

But there is a happy ending, as Buttercup had two babies: one was a filly named Woodstock Norths Cosmopolitan Girl (Cosmo), and the other was a gorgeous appaloosa colt named Woodstock Norths Whos

Appy Now (Appy), who looks exactly like her, and I had sold both of them. Their new owners gave the ultimate sacrifice and sold both of them back to me, so I have both her son and daughter now and they are running in the pasture where my darling Buttercup once roamed, and they are keeping her memory alive in our hearts.

We will be breeding the two of them in the spring and we will have Buttercup's grandbaby here to love, and she (as somehow I know it will be a she) will be named Sister Goldenhair, and my darling Buttercup will have her memory alive in our hearts for as long as we live. I can now envision her running through the pasture whinnying to me and running to me, and even though her ashes are right by my bedside, she will always be in my heart; and her ashes will be buried with me.

For all of you who read this, please treasure your horses and give them all the love that you can, as you may not get another chance.

The Great Escape

By Kim Sterchi
Sierra Ranch
Grass Valley, California
SierraMinis@aol.com

It was 5:00 a.m. and the Breeder Alert was beeping away. I fumbled around in the dark until I found the annoying little black box and shut it off. With mixed emotions, I flew out of bed to check on Teka. She is our tri-colored mare who was expecting at the time. The beam of light from my flashlight scanned the large paddock. Finally the light came to rest on Teka, who was lying flat on her side with her legs stretched out. I was delighted when I threw my clothes on to rush outside, because I would be leaving in a few hours for the first show of the season, and hoped Teka would foal before I left.

I had approached the paddock quietly, observing Teka as she lay on her side straining. She seemed fine. She casually got up and down a few times. However, no sac had appeared yet and I was beginning to get a little nervous. It was a moonless night, so the beam from my flashlight illuminated the pretty pinto mare.

Many minutes passed and finally I could wait no longer. There may be a problem, I thought, and I would have to examine her. After scrubbing and donning a shoulder-length glove, I waited for the next opportunity to palpate her. I was alone with no one to hold her, so I had to be careful. Finally, she lay down again and began to strain. I had been helping mares foal for 17 years, so I felt relatively comfortable with what I was about to do.

I was in the middle of the examination when the mare suddenly jumped up and took off. The puzzling part was that I had not felt anything at all!

I called the veterinarian. I explained how she had all the obvious signs of labor, yet nothing was happening and nearly an hour had gone by. He felt that if I had not felt the foal, even in a partial exam, then her cervix must still be closed. It was possible that she was in transition. I did not feel comfortable with his opinion, so after I hung up the phone, I called another veterinarian. He basically felt the same—transition.

I was not satisfied with either of their responses, so I went back to Teka to perform another internal examination. It was starting to get light out and Teka was standing quietly, occasionally looking at her sides. She was calm—too calm. Instead of her labor progressing, she was getting more comfortable. I wondered what in the world was happening. I tied her to the fence and began to palpate her. She was going to have no part of it and fought me to the point that I felt I had better back off. I still felt no baby. Over two hours had gone by and Teka was showing very few signs now that a baby was impending. I thought either the veterinarians were right or we were dealing with a false pregnancy.

Teka was resting quietly so I decided to take a shower and get ready to leave for the show. Help would be arriving soon and I would decide what to do then. While in the house, I glanced out the window toward the north pasture to see a sight I will never forget. The entire herd of 25 broodmares was stampeding across the hillside. A tiny seal brown colt with his head held high looked as if he was leading the entire herd. He was running as fast as his little legs could carry him and a young mare was quick on his heels. Knowing that the colt was probably in more trouble than he appeared, I raced to his rescue. It did not take long to capture the feisty little colt and young mare. However, it took even less time to determine that this was not that young mare's foal. I couldn't believe what I began to think. Could he be Teka's baby? If so, how did he get through two fences to get into the north pasture? And, most importantly, when was he born?

As soon as I introduced Teka and the foal, my first question was answered. With a quick nuzzle, the two became inseparable. I sat back and pondered the remaining questions that I had. Why was Teka not upset when she foaled and the baby disappeared? That was easy. This was Teka's first live foal. She had two previous full-term pregnancies and had lost them both. So, it was natural to have her baby taken from her at birth. She must have foaled right on the fence line, which enabled the baby to get up on the wrong side of the fence (no pun intended). How the baby got through the second fence and into the north pasture will always be a mystery.

I checked the paddock again and found afterbirth in the corner under some straw. It was easily missed in the dark. Apparently, Teka must have had the foal and was recovering when the Breeder Alert went off. I only wish I could have witnessed how this little colt survived his first several hours of life by himself. Considering the events that took place, we affectionately named him "Houdini."

Mini Horses...
What Are They Good For?

What are *sunsets* good for?
To see one's flamboyant colors
splashed across a somber skyline
makes my heart leap up!

What are Mini Horses good for?
To see happy foals cavorting
just outside my kitchen window
makes my heart leap up!

What are *redbirds* good for?
To hear one pour its tiny heart out
in a joyous burst of song
makes my spirit soar!

What are Mini Horses good for?
To hear joyous, high-pitched nickers
greet me from across the pasture
makes my spirit soar!

What are *breezes* good for?
To feel a cool one's sudden gust
across my sweaty, sunburned brow,
gives me pause for joy.

What are Mini Horses good for?
To feel pushy little muzzles
search my pockets for a sweet treat
gives me pause for joy.

What are *wild roses* good for?
To walk old fence rows where they flourish
and drink in their fragile fragrance
satisfies my soul!

What are Mini Horses good for?
To wrap my arms around my mini
and drink in its horse aroma
satisfies my soul!

By Jody Chenoweth
Chenterra Farm Miniature Horses
Leavenworth, Kansas
www.smallhorse.com/farm/chenterra

The Little Filly Who Could

By Joanne and Larry Ross
Scott Creek Miniature Horse Farm
Salem, Oregon
www.scottcreek.com

In order to put some credibility to this story we have to endure a short mathematics lesson to verify the gestation period of the foal. First of all, most resources state that horses foal within a range of 320 to 360 days after the foal is conceived. For miniature horses, we use the following formula: Breeding date – 35 days = projected foaling date.

The mare in question had foaled on April 7. Our records indicated that she was rebred on April 23 through May 1. In June we had the mare ultrasounded. At that time she was verified in foal. Based on the size of the pregnancy the veterinarian estimated the breeding date to be April 29 to May 1. Using our formula, one would expect that by subtracting 35 days from May 1, the intended foaling date should be approximately March 25. This date had to be correct since she had just given birth and had bred back on her first heat cycle after foaling.

Mom's Big Problem

At about nine months of pregnancy, we always get a little edgy in anticipation of the foaling season and start watching the mares very closely. Shortly after January 1, we came out one morning to feed. We found this mare down in the loafing shed. She was not in labor. We determined this since she was not showing signs of uterine contractions. There were no fetal membranes protruding from her vulva. There was no telltale smell of amniotic fluid on her tail. She did show signs of diarrhea. She could hardly stand up, even when prodded. When we finally did get her up, she barely walked and was highly disoriented. It reminded us of our cow when it had "milk fever" (phosphorus/calcium imbalance). The previous night, the mare had shown no outward signs of problems. We immediately rushed the mare to the Oregon State University Veterinary Teaching Hospital.

Had it not been for the outstanding diagnostic skills, emergency room techniques, and aggressive treatment regimen by the staff at the vet school, there is no doubt we would have lost this mare. Due to her diarrhea and resulting loss of fluids, the mare's body chemistry was seriously out of balance. This in itself was life-threatening, and also accounted for the reason the mare was unable to coordinate walking. We also found blood in the mare's stool, which was very alarming. As we left the mare in the hands of the vet school, we were warned that her condition was life-threatening and that the chance for aborting her foal was extremely high.

The mare spent two weeks at the vet school. She was diagnosed with Necrotizing Colitis. This is an inflammation of the colon in which the lining of the bowel actually starts sloughing off, causing the horse to bleed from the rectum. No actual cause of the colitis was ever pinpointed. We returned to pick up the mare, who had lost a little weight as a result of the ordeal; but was amazingly still carrying her foal. It was now mid-January.

The Surprise

We were starting to watch the expectant mares from the closed-circuit cameras in the barn each night. During foaling season, this becomes a major ordeal. While you are staring at the same picture on the monitor for endless days, you become a little punchy and come up with crazy names for these programs, such as "General Stall Watch" or "Days of Our Mares." On February 4th, about 5 a.m., Joanne wandered down to the barn to take a first-hand look at one of the mares under the camera. She had been acting a little curiously. Everything was fine there. As she headed back, she peeked into the stall where our recuperating mare was. Much to her amazement, she was greeted by an itty-bitty black pinto foal standing (well, sort of), dried off, attempting to nurse on her mother.

After suffering a few moments of paralysis, Joanne's neurons started functioning on overtime. The first, fleeting thought was, how could I have miscalculated. The second, it's alive, let's get down to business. Treat the umbilical stump with Nolvasan. Blanket the foal to help her conserve body heat. Check the mare to assure the placenta has passed and to assure she has milk. Check the foal to observe if it is nursing aggressively.

Oh, boy! Here's a problem. Either the foal has an exceptional appetite or the mare is dry. Upon feeling the mare's udder, Joanne discovered that it was completely flat. This is highly abnormal for a mare with a newborn foal. Joanne was unable to strip any milk from the nipples. The foal was constantly trying to nurse. This wouldn't seem reasonable with a newborn foal who was getting its fill. It became very clear that this foal had not received any nourishment since birth. Since we had not witnessed the birth, it was difficult to tell how long the foal had been alive. It was standing and its hair coat was dry, so we estimated that it had been a number of hours since foaling.

Deep Trouble

All foals are essentially born on the verge of critical condition unless Mother Nature's steps proceed in order. It is imperative that newborns receive nourishment soon after birth for two very important reasons: (1) Foals are essentially born in an energy-deficit situation. They have very few reserves of energy to maintain body heat and carry out bodily functions. Without "groceries" from mom or another source within the first few hours of life, foals start showing signs of bodily stress and depression. (2) Mother's first milk (colostrum) provides antibodies (infection fighters). Foals are born with an immature immune system that is not yet fully functioning. The foal does not have antibodies in its bloodstream to fight off infectious organisms that are constantly present in the air we breathe, for example. If the foal does not receive antibodies through the mare's colostrum within the first 6-12 hours of life, it will not have resistance to common infections such as pneumonia, influenza, tetanus, and other common diseases. Without these defenses, the foal will more than likely perish within a short period of time after birth.

Normally we "bank" colostrum by saving a small percentage produced by each mare, then freeze it. Unfortunately, due to an extended power outage for a period of days we had lost our supply. We had no choice but to rush the foal to the OSU Vet School.

Upon arriving, the filly was examined. The vital signs were taken. Blood was drawn for evaluation. We discussed what had occurred so far. When we told the OSU staff this filly was approximately six weeks premature, there was an additional element of alarm. We figured her gestation had only been 281 to 282 days. OSU stated that foals surviving that were this premature was almost unheard of. Much like with premature humans, under-development of the lungs and insufficient surfactant in the lungs can lead to major respiratory complications.

Shortly after we got to the vet school, the filly began to lose her vitality. Since she had not received any nourishment, her little fire had started to go out. She lost her suckling reflex. She did not want to stand on her own. Her temperature began dropping. Fortunately, by a combination of keeping her warm on a heating pad, tube-feeding her a commercial milk replacer, and IV feeding, she pulled through that crisis and recovered her strength and will to live.

Plasma, Antibodies, and the Waiting Game

Since the mare was dry and no colostrum was available, the vet school decided to perform a plasma transfusion to the foal. This is a procedure where donor horses are highly immunized against all forms of diseases. A small portion of their blood is then harvested. The plasma portion of the blood is extracted and stored for later uses such as with our foal. The plasma, packed with antibodies, is then intravenously transfused slowly into the foal's bloodstream. This plasma mingles with the foal's blood and the antibodies then provide a defense against infection until the foal's immune system fully develops and produces adequate antibodies to protect itself. When we left the vet school, the foal was looking somewhat revived from when we had brought her in. That was encouraging. The veterinarians reminded us, however, that the situation with her lungs was serious and that she was, by no means, out of the woods.

The filly spent two weeks in the vet hospital. As warned, she developed pneumonia. Through aggressive antibiotic treatment and constant monitoring, she pulled through the ordeal very well. The filly weighed approximately 14 lbs. when we had taken her to OSU. When she was released, two weeks later, she had gained one pound. She was taking the bottle vigorously every two hours. Her vital signs were stable. Her bloodwork was looking satisfactory. We felt pretty good about that, given the numerous problems that she had fought her way through.

Feeding the Bottomless Pit

Suffice it to say, it would be hard to find anything much more demanding than an orphaned foal. We built a tiny stall in our bedroom. She was constantly jumping out of the stall to chase us around the house. Our feeding schedule of every two hours was not acceptable to her. She would wake us up in the middle of the night nickering from her stall when she was hungry.

The foal did not seem, at first, to be taking in an adequate amount of groceries. The resources we have read state that newborns should consume between 15% and 25% of their body weight per day in milk. The commercial milk replacer was not a hit. She was not consuming close to this level of food, so we were getting concerned about malnutrition. We had heard about raising horses on goat's milk. Fortunately we had a milk goat farm down the road. When the filly got a taste of this, she was like an entirely different animal. She became ravenous. It seemed like she would drink as much milk as we would put in front of her. We fed her at two-hour intervals around the clock. Her weight shot up. Her energy shot up. We became a little concerned and were careful to keep her intake between the 15-25% parameters per day, as we had read. We had to be concerned about regularity of bowel movements. The filly appeared to become constipated occasionally. We were forced in a couple of instances to use an enema after an extended period of constipation.

The Nurse Mare

We maintained this regimen for approximately one month. We were introducing the filly to grain and alfalfa leaves in her stall. She was taken out daily in the hopes of stimulating her to eat grass. Since we were not very good about demonstrating grazing techniques, she wasn't making much progress.

We heard of a mare that had just lost a foal. We contacted the owners. The mare had not had a chance to bond with the foal. They graciously consented to allow us to attempt to graft our foal onto their mare. The mare was very receptive and immediately claimed our foal as her own. Our foal had some difficulty figuring out how to nurse from the mare. We had to bottle feed her for a couple of days until she was getting all of her nourishment from the mare. The situation worked out very well all the way around because the foal was then provided with herd experiences that she would otherwise not have received by being hand-raised. We, of course, were also relieved from the major burden of feeding and caring for the totally demanding foal.

Emergency Nourishment

We learned a number of things from this experience. The one critical care tidbit that we will always remember is that if we have a foal that has not nursed, we will definitely get food into it as soon as possible. In this case, the mare was the first to foal of the year and we had no other mares to milk. As stated, we had no colostrum to give.

Scott Creek
Fashionable Miss Tique.

The veterinary resources we have consulted since this incident give a formula for "fortified milk": 8 oz. 2% cow's milk + 1 tsp. Karo syrup. If we were in this situation again, we would mix this up and give some to the foal as we were heading to the vet school. Obviously, this is only to provide the newborn with nourishment to keep the fire going on an emergency basis. This formula does nothing to account for immune deficiency or other problems.

As it turned out, this filly, after all of her trials, has flourished. We never cease to be amazed by the heart and will to live these horses have when given a reasonable opportunity and there is a good working relationship between the horse owner and the treating veterinarians.

Postscript: Miss Tique went to live with a lovely schoolteacher on the east coast of the U.S. Tique is the farm greeter and classroom favorite. I just received a notice that Miss Tique's first filly foal won national champion futurity and national champion open halter yearling filly at the AMHR national show in September 2001.

"Easter Ears"

By Penny Lary
Patty Cake Ranch
Dallas, Texas
www.pattycakeranch.com.

"MOM!!!" My 16-year-old daughter shrieked as she raced inside the house, slamming the door behind her.

"Ohmigosh, Alyssa! What's wrong?!" (I was sure the news must be very bad.)

"Mom! My counselor called me into her office right before last period, and I'm three hours short on my community service! I gotta do something NOW or I'll get an incomplete for the whole semester! What if I don't graduate?!"

After a few tense, tearful, and no doubt life-altering moments, I managed to calm her down. Sometimes it's hard for teenagers to grasp the utter insignificance of what to me was a fairly hurdle-less problem. Completely unlike, say, dieting.

"Can you perform this three hours of community service any-where?" I asked.

Alyssa showed me a copy of a pre-approved list which had been posted for weeks. Not surprisingly, however, almost every project on the list had been taken by other, slightly more organized and foresight-ful students.

As we pored over the list, one possible recipient caught my atten-tion: a low-income day-care center in the heart of downtown Dallas. "How about this?" I asked.

"What on earth would I do there for three hours? Babysit? Don't they already have people to do that? Isn't that what a day-care place does?"

I admitted she had a point.

Nevertheless, an idea began to form. "How about this, Alyssa? What if you took one of the minis to the center? I'll bet the kids would absolutely love to have a little horse to pet and learn about for the afternoon."

Suddenly I was on a roll.

Swelling with fresh, creative ideas, I effused: "And not only that, it's so close to Easter, maybe I could make an outfit for him to wear, like a hat of some sort, with bunny ears sticking up, that said Happy Easter."

"Easter Ears." I liked it!

Alyssa agreed, and after some high-level strategic research, like where to find horse-butt-sized rubber pants for the car trip, the plan was in place.

Soon the designated day arrived. Alyssa and her best friend, Elizabeth, got to leave school right after lunch. They headed home to retrieve the little Easter Bunny...er, mini horse...before setting off downtown to selflessly perform their community service.

Alyssa and colt at a Dallas day-care center.

I guess when we were brainstorming it must have sounded easier, and tidier, to transport a horse in the back of a Suburban to an indoor, inner-city activity. But, bottom-line, it wasn't my graduation requirement...I was just the idea person...the mini-provider...the Easter-Ear manufacturer. Well, and the Suburban owner. I helped the girls take out the third seat and cover the entire back floor of the truck with a large green tarp.

Maybe the colt would think he was riding on grass.

We put on his blue visor I'd decorated that said "Happy Easter," with the large, pink bunny ears attached. I braided and twirled the colt's tail into a tight little ball and wrapped it snugly with a white elastic leg bandage. I topped it off with a huge wad of cotton. Sticking out through the rubber pants, it passed pretty well for a bunny tail. Alyssa drove off down the street, Elizabeth riding "shotgun" (or maybe "pooperscoop"), with the colt facing backward, staring out the rear window.

Just another ordinary afternoon. Doesn't everyone do this?

How the girls handled themselves and their funny-hat-rubber-pant-wearing-bunny-tailed-Easter-Eared-charge was now up to them. I anxiously awaited their return from the day-care center. I didn't know what to expect. I thought it could be interesting.

Later, Alyssa reported that 40 little kids, aged toddler to ten, had the time of their lives. They pointed, petted, pulled, pounded, played, and poked—eyes, ears, nose, teeth, tail…under the tail—anything they could get their hands on, up to, around, or in. Beyond hyperactive. Noise levels approaching a civil defense warning. And the questions!

"Where do little kids come up with this stuff? Mom, they asked *everything*!"

"How'd you handle the answers?"

"One kid wouldn't quit pestering us with these really embarrassing questions. I didn't know what to say. Elizabeth was no help. Her face was beet red!"

"What'd ya do?"

"I tried everything to change the subject. Finally, I tried bribing him. I told the kid if he'd quit asking those questions, I'd let him wear the visor with the Easter Ears for the rest of the afternoon."

My little girl was growing up. She'll make a great mom some day.

A Mother's Day Miracle

By Elaine Jones
Jones' Mini Whinnies
West Middlesex, Pennsylvania
http://jonesminiwhinnies.homestead.com/home.html

On May 13th, 2000, we had a show in New Jersey. It was a great show, and we headed home shortly after noon. I had to stop at Galloping G's to pick up a mare on the way so it was an extremely long trip, but I knew I had to get home. It was around midnight when I got home and needless to say, I was exhausted.

David helped me unload the horses and I went to check the mares. Sure enough, Honey was waiting for me to get home. No sleep for me! I waited with her until around 3 a.m. and labor began. I had delivered many babies from Honey, but this delivery was different. The sac was there, but nothing was in it. I was getting nervous as she was working so hard, and it didn't seem she was getting very far. I decided to open the sac and help. I pulled. She pushed. The legs were there but right with the head. They would not stretch out. Suddenly it seemed to pop. We both worked real hard. Then as I got the head out, I knew why. It was a dwarf.

Twenty years of breeding miniature horses, and we got our first dwarf. I was so upset. I was one of those narrow-minded people who said, "I would never keep a dwarf." I sat and debated about taking it outside but I didn't have the heart. Honey turned to look at her new baby and quickly looked back at the wall with a blank stare. She did this twice as if she knew something was wrong. With her other babies you could witness the bonding immediately. This was different for both of us. I decided to go to bed and let nature take its course.

In the morning, I reluctantly went to the barn, scared that I would find a dead baby that couldn't stand or nurse. As I looked in Honey's stall, I saw the proudest mommy of all and a little grey baby sucking up all the milk she could get. I told Honey, "If you can accept this, I can too." After all, it was Mother's Day morning .

I spoke to some friends and told them what we got, and I said we have to find her a home quick. Within two weeks, we had a deposit on her. We planned to keep her until we could wean her and then she would go. She did need a name and since she seemed like a little misfit we decided we would call her Missy for "misfit." Little did we know what a blessing she would be.

Missy.

Missy was different, all right. She was a little bundle of love. She ran loose most of the time and grew on all of us.

Then the nightmares started. Every night I would wake up crying because I was dreaming that it was the day that Missy was to leave us. I couldn't function during the day because I just kept trying to think how I could get out of this mess. I couldn't tell the little boy that was counting on Missy being his pet that he couldn't have her now. Then I got the idea to find him another dwarf. So, I made some phone calls and I found one and I returned the deposit with a note of apology. What a relief!

Missy will stay with us for as long as she lives. We know that God sent us a special little blessing on that wonderful Mother's Day morning. And we are extremely grateful.

Bobbi's Story

By Dona Neargarder
Kickapoo Acres
Fletcher, Ohio
http://kickapoo-acres.virtualave.net

I first met "Bobbi" when she was six years old. Her grandmother had called and wanted to know if she could bring her granddaughter to see my minis…and being a "proud parent" type, and always eager to show off my "babies" to everyone remotely interested, I said, "Of course, come on out!"

When they arrived, I was expecting to see a bright-eyed, excited little girl. I was not prepared for what I saw when the door of the car opened. There was a "small for her years," very quiet, expressionless child. She had the biggest, brownest eyes that sadly didn't even show a hint of excitement…and, oh yes, crutches.

You see, Bobbi has Spina Bifida. My heart went out to this tiny slip of a girl as she struggled, very determinedly, to cross the lawn to my barn alongside her grandmother.

After asking Bobbi several questions to get acquainted, and only getting blank stares in return, her grandmother quietly confided in me that Bobbi had not spoken since her beloved grandfather (with whom she was very close) had died. I was so touched by this beautiful, sad little girl, I wanted to hold her, but knew she would only resist such familiarity with a virtual stranger. So, with tears welling in my eyes, I continued to talk to Bobbi and explained to her and her grandmother all about the miniature horse breed and introduced them to all my horses by name. For some reason, Bobbi took an instant liking to my 27" yearling silver dapple stallion, "Kickapoo's Nickelodeon."

When I brought "Nick" out of the stall for Bobbi to see him better, she released her grip on one of her crutches and reached out with one tiny, pink-polished finger and proceeded to touch his spots, one by one, as if counting them. Her eyes were as big as saucers as she ran her shaky hand over his long silvery mane, then up to the points of his ears, over his eyelashes, and down to his velvety soft nose. All the while, Nick remained motionless as if in a trance. Then all at once, Bobbi surprised us by dropping her crutches and taking Nick's lead from my hand. By leaning against the stalls for support, and literally dragging each foot, inches at a time, Bobbi proceeded to lead Nick up and down the aisleway in the barn. I quickly searched Bobbi's grandmother's face for a sign of worry, but found a look of surprised delight instead. Nick was intuitively gentle with this quiet little girl, who was acting as if she had all the strength and power in the world, but actually could barely stand.

Bobbi's grandmother and I were truly amazed at what we were watching, and finally (for fear of Bobbi tiring too much) convinced her that Nick had been walked enough, and it was time to put him back into his stall. I reached for the lead, but Bobbi would have none of that. She stared into my eyes with a look of stubborn persistence, and pulled the lead away from my reach. She continued to support herself against the walls, and not only lead Nick back into his stall, but also unsnapped the lead from his halter, shut his stall door and made sure it was latched—all by herself! By this time, I felt almost "privileged" to be witnessing a very unique and personal "bonding" between my little stallion and one very special little girl.

Bobbi with "Nick" during her first visit to Kickapoo Acres.

After that day, Bobbi and her family became regular visitors to my farm, coming to see each new foal as it arrived in the spring, and followed me and my horses to local shows and parades whenever they could to cheer us on. I anxiously anticipated each visit and the possibility of maybe hearing Bobbi speak for the first time. As she would make her way through the barn to Nick's stall, I would repeatedly ask her questions, always searching her cherub face for any indications of forthcoming speech. But she always remained silent, preferring to "speak" with her eyes. (She had a way with communicating with her grandmother with her eyes and hands, and it amazed me how her grandmother always seemed to know what Bobbi was "saying.") But once in a while, I thought I could see a hint of a smile on that little stone face, especially when she stopped by her little buddy, Nick. Or was it just my imagination?

Eventually, they decided to breed their 40" pony, Cindy, to my miniature stallion to possibly get a mini-sized pony for Bobbi. This was no small feat, by any means, and required digging a hole to stand the mare in so my small stallion could reach her. After several attempts, we accomplished it, and to Bobbi's delight, the following spring Cindy foaled a beautiful little sorrel filly with a large star and four white socks. Bobbi decided on the name "Honeysuckle" for her filly (because she was the color of honey). Bobbi works with Honeysuckle daily by supporting herself on the fence with one hand as she leads with the other, and maneuvers her uncooperative feet in between! And she is already asking when they can get a baby from Honeysuckle!

Yes…I said "*asking*," because just recently Bobbi began talking again! Only to people who are very close to her, and most times it's just a whisper into her grandmother's ear–but it's a start! I know there is probably some technical, psychological explanation for this, and I feel that Bobbi's very loving and supportive family had a lot to do with it. But I also choose to believe that the minis played a significant part in reaching Bobbi's emotional hiding place and bringing her out of her sadness so she could again smile and enjoy life and all the joys of just being a little girl.

Bobbi, so far in her short life, has endured countless operations to help her be mobile, and not restricted to a wheelchair, and she takes them all in stride, like a little trooper. In fact, she has now started riding lessons on her pony, Cindy; and she is hoping to someday be able to show Honeysuckle by herself. Bobbi is a very determined and courageous little girl who I feel very lucky to know, and I wish her a life filled with smiles, happiness and of course…little horses.

The Short Life of Seastar

By Jonita Smith
Rocky Creek Miniatures
Haslet, Texas
RCMinis817@aol.com

Star, one of my best mares, was due to foal and I watched very carefully every minute, night and day, waiting for the excitement to come. What is it going to be, boy or girl? What color? Sorrel, black, bay, gray, buckskin, appaloosa or pinto? Would it arrive without problems? Do I have everything ready for the new life? You know the things that always go through your mind as you impatiently await the big event.

Finally, on April 25, 2001, at 1:50 a.m., Star foaled the most beautiful, healthy, little sorrel filly with a perfect star on her forehead. We named her Seastar because you could "see" a star. It was a good easy birth for mom. Thank God! Seastar developed quite a personality. Very full of life and nosy as could be. I wanted to try to breed Star back on foal heat, so I took her to a friend's to be bred. That night Seastar seemed to be a little laid back and quiet; I thought she was just a little stressed from going on a trailer ride and being in new surroundings.

The next day she seemed a little more stressed and lethargic. On May 6th, I had to go out of town that day and my friend who owned the stallion Star was being bred to, called the vet and he (the vet) suggested to get her in as soon as possible, so off she went to the vet's office. Blood was drawn and tests were done, only to find out dreadful news! Seastar had a rare blood disorder where her mom and her dad's blood did not mix well together. Similar to the Rh factor in humans. The hope was slim but I had to take a chance on saving her life.

The vet tried to cleanse her blood, take out some old blood and give her new. Only time would tell. To everyone's surprise, she managed to be pulling through this mess and was getting a little stronger for a day or two, and then would get weak again. After about ten days, she seemed to show really good steady signs of being better and could quite possibly come home that coming weekend. Everyone at the vet's office had fallen in love with this little girl. She was quite something! She had the best veterinarian care possible and was watched and monitored with extreme care for almost two weeks. We made daily visits to her to see her and to talk to her and her mom.

On the evening of May 18th, Seastar took a turn for the worse and by the 19th we were informed that she would not be able to pull out of it this time. We were sadly asked for permission to let her go. The dreadful decision had to be made to put this little beauty down. Everyone tried desperately to save her, including Seastar herself, but it just was out of our hands.

We love you dearly, Seastar.
April 25-May 19, 2001.

A Mini Story

By Barbara Gartman
Little Thicket Miniature Horse Ranch
Scurry, Texas

The State Fair of Texas was bustling with excited fairgoers as they wandered from building to building. I was one of those people a dozen years ago.

Strolling through the animal barns was something my husband and I enjoyed. The musty smell of hay mixed with animals and people added to the thrill of seeing cages and cages of small animals. Then we went into another barn and there was the prettiest, most thrilling sight I had ever seen: a tiny horse, not more than 30" tall. This was my first encounter with a mini and I fell in love with the little horses almost immediately.

We continued to stroll and look at all the different little horses, pintos, dapples, palominos, all just like their larger cousins. I asked my husband, Glenn, "Please, let's get one." He was very logical and since we lived in Arlington, in the city, he answered with a definite "No."

Still, my teenage son and I wanted to see more of these little half-pint horses. We called the American Miniature Horse Association and asked for the closest location of anyone raising miniatures in our area. Since I thought "half-pint" was such a cute description, a dealer, Half-Pint Miniatures, caught my eye. After making an appointment, my son Tom and I went out to see what she had. A silver dapple filly called Dewdrop came up to us. She was so loving and irresistible. My son hugged her neck. I brushed her with a grooming brush close by. How could anyone turn down such a lovable animal? But I did. I explained my husband's thoughts and told her we lived in the city. She remarked that since Tom was in FFA it could be his project, then the city wouldn't complain. I began to weaken. After all, what she said was true. Tom started in the usual, "I'll take care of her, Mom. You'll never have to clean after her."

There still wasn't enough money in the household budget to pay her asking price. She had another suggestion: "You can pay her out."

Dewdrop and Tom.

Wow! All the problems were solved. I made a down payment, promised to come by every couple of weeks to feed, brush and get acquainted with our little baby. Yep, all the problems were solved—except one.

After I got home that evening, I put the proposition to my husband once again. "Don't be silly, we only have a 50 by 150-foot lot and it has a house on it."

Well, we kept our promise. Twice a month Tom and I would go over and play with our little baby. I would give the lady the agreed payment and we would run out to pet, brush and play with our little Dewdrop. And each time we would go home and talk again about Tom needing an FFA project for the coming year, how great it would be to have a miniature horse and all the nice things we could think of to convince Glenn how much we needed a miniature.

Time went on and one day, we paid the lady as usual and then went out to play and pet our baby. In a few minutes the lady came out of the house smiling, with a big brown envelope in her hand.

"Here," she said. "Here are the papers on your horse. She's all paid for and I need the room for the new babies I have coming. You can take her home today."

Whoops! We didn't even own a trailer. In fact, we didn't even know anyone who had one. Tom and I looked at each other. A big grin spread across his face, and I guess, mine too, because the lady began to laugh. We took one look at how small Dewdrop was and another at the nice space behind the rear seat of our Ford station wagon. The papers went in the front seat, Tom in the middle set of seats, so he could hold Dewdrop who rode all the way home in the back of the station wagon.

When Glenn came in from work, I spread my arms and said, "Honey, I need you to build me a pen about this big."

Wide-eyed, he said, "What have you done now?"

Well, he fussed a little when he saw her, but it wasn't long before he was brushing and petting her too. Miniatures don't grow tall; they just grow big in your heart.

Surviving Rising Waters
(or, E-mail from a Friend)

by Darwin Parker
Darro Miniature Horse Farm
Houston, Texas
dwparker@pdq.net

"Hello Lady,

"I finally got back up on a computer after we had three feet of water in our house from the flooding in June. No, I didn't lose the new filly in my back yard you asked about, but there were some real scary moments, let me tell you.

"It'd been raining already for several days. We kept thinking it would quit, but it just kept raining and raining. Remember I told you I had brought the new filly and her momma up from the pasture to the house because the baby was so tiny? She's a beauty and I wanted to keep a real close eye on her.

"Well, it never quit raining. After a while the water started accumulating in patches on the lawn. Then, pretty soon we started to worry that if there was no place for the water to drain, it could come up to the house.

"We weren't actually scared yet even though it was still raining, and dark in the middle of the day.

"Then we thought it would probably be better bein' safe than sorry, so my mom started gathering up some things from the house. Next thing we knew, there was water actually in the house! At first it was only a couple of inches. Then it started rising real fast! All of a sudden we were knee deep in water in the house! I shouted to Mom to go out front and get in the truck, and I raced out back to get the horses.

"I could tell the filly and her momma were soaked to the skin and scared to death. The water was nearly up to the filly's belly where they were standing on one side of the yard. I waded over to where they were huddled up together. Rain was hittin' me hard in the face. I grabbed the filly and kinda threw her up on my shoulders, with her legs straddling either side of my head. I took two little legs in each hand and started wading back through the house and out to the truck.

"This was all happening so fast. A few more seconds and I swear that baby woulda been swept away in the flood like a cricket down a creek.

"I got to the trailer, put the filly in, and waded back to get more animals. By now the water was well up over my knees. It was thundering and lightning and the rain was blowing real hard. My mom was shoutin' for me and my brother to find the other animals and get 'em in

The filly that almost washed away.

the truck and trailer. Some of the animals needed special food and medication. We wanted to get that and horse food and some clothes and emergency supplies for us because we didn't know how long we'd have to be gone.

"Three times we waded back into the house, with water up to our chests in some parts. It was tough going. But something just kept moving me forward, like I didn't have a choice. I just couldn't take time to think about whether this was a good idea or not. I was getting the rest of my animals and what we all needed, and that was that!

"I must have been pumpin' pure adrenaline. Somehow we managed to gather up all the animals and enough supplies, get everything into the truck and trailer, and then drive a ways to higher ground. Water was everywhere, churning and swirling around. It was awful, and dark. Very dark. Then it got real quiet, and all you could hear was the water, lapping up over the truck tires.

"My mom, my brother and I spent that Friday night in my truck with all the animals in the horse trailer. We had four dogs, three mares, and the little filly. It kept on raining, but not as hard as it had been. All that night I kept wading back to the trailer to check on the filly and make sure the water wasn't clear up over her. She was smaller than the dogs.

"You know what? If I'd had to, I'd have held that filly in my lap and tried driving the truck out through the flood waters. I kept wondering if this is what Noah must have felt like on the Ark.

"Then Saturday morning around 8:00 a.m., the rain stopped and the sun came out. After a while the water went down enough below the front bumper that I was able to drive out. I went to a parking lot a few blocks down the road where it was very high and dry. I parked the front of the truck on a slant so the water in the trailer could drain out. After that I was able to feed the dogs and horses some breakfast. We all looked like red-eyed drowned rats. We spent the rest of Saturday pretty much in a daze.

"Sunday my brothers and I decided it was time to go back and check out the house. We didn't even know if we could get back into it, but we wanted to try before we let Mom see it. When we got there the water was gone, but so was virtually everything else. The physical structure was standing, but everything was either covered in mud or just plain gone, ruined or washed away. 50 years of stuff. 50 years of memories. I couldn't believe it, and I knew Mom would be heartbroken.

"But you know, as bad as this was, and it was real bad, at least we had each other, and the animals. I guess when it's a choice between saving your family, or saving your stuff, it's really not a choice at all…you just do what you gotta do and pray that God grants you more time with your loved ones. All of us made it, except for one of the dogs. She'd drunk some of the flood water which must have been contaminated. Her kidneys shut down, and we lost her. But at least she was with us when it happened and not swept away somewhere all alone in all that water.

"So now we've started the long task of cleanup, and yes, that's hell, and yes, we lost everything material, but, like I said, if it turns out that you and those close to you make it through, you know you haven't really lost anything. God's given you a gift of what's most important in this earthly life: more time to spend with your family and friends, human and animal!

"Take care, Lady. Love your family and friends. Thank God for each and every day, and never forget to hug your dogs and horses.

"Your buddy & almost lost friend, Darwin."

My Little Star

By Lisa Foster
Country Hills Miniature Horses
Reeds Spring, Missouri
http://countryhillsminihorses.homestead.com/

I have owned animals most of my life, whether it was a dog, cat or a big horse. I also have lost some of these pets over the years.

In all my life I never thought I could love any animal as much as I did my first miniature horse. Her name was Little Star.

I had wanted a miniature horse for years, but my husband and two children and I lived in a subdivision, so we were not able to have horses. So six years ago we built our dream home. We own five acres, most of which we keep mowed and that is our yard. My in-laws own a couple hundred acres around us and we are high up on a hill. My husband and I and my in-laws are the only ones that live up here, so we do not have to worry about traffic, etc.

Well, five years ago I finally got a chance to buy my first miniature. We didn't have a lot of money because we had just built our home the year before and we were raising two children. In my mind I knew what I wanted. I wanted a red miniature with a white mane and tail. I don't know why, but I turned down pintos, etc. in our area. We also know how expensive miniatures can be. This was before we had the Internet, so I called all over trying to find the color I wanted and I also knew I wanted a little girl. I probably could have bought a more expensive miniature for what we paid in phone bills for two months!

Anyway, I finally found a farm in Crescent, OK that had a little red filly with a white mane and tail for only $500. The only problem was her mother would not nurse her so they were bottle feeding her. She also had back leg problems; she walked almost on the back of her hooves. But, I didn't care, she sounded like just what I wanted.

After several phone calls, I finally convinced the farm that even though I had never owned a miniature I could take good care of her.

Now, she was five hours away. So I had to break the news to my husband that I finally found the one I wanted. We could not afford a transporter and we didn't have a trailer. We had just bought a new van in August; I bought Little Star in November. My husband knew this was something I had really wanted for a very long time. So he took the two back seats out of our new van and put a tarp down, and on a Saturday morning he and my dad left to go pick up my new filly. That was the longest day—the time went by so slow! But, that evening, here they pulled in my driveway and opened the back of the van. That was the prettiest little horse I had ever seen in my life. I can't even explain the feelings I had. And she had a white star on her forehead, so that is how she got her name—Little Star.

Lisa's Granny (Edna) Owens bottle-feeding Little Star.

My dad and my husband still laugh about the trip. They said they stopped for lunch at a Wendy's and were a little embarrassed going through the drive-through with a little horse people could see through the windows of the van.

Anyway, here she was, eight weeks old. The owner had sent me her Foal-Lac powder, and four times a day I would mix the powder and put it in a regular baby bottle and feed her. We went through plenty of baby nipples. She even got to where all I had to do was shake that bottle and she came running, she knew that sound! I cut her bottle feedings down and finally weaned her from her bottle at almost five months. I think I would have fed her that bottle forever, but everyone kept telling me it was time to break her. I knew it, but she loved that little baby bottle.

At about three months old, our vet put splints on her legs. My dad taught my husband how to trim feet and so he worked hard keeping her feet trimmed. By the time she was a year old her back legs were almost perfect, and by two years old they were.

I had never realized how smart miniature horses are. I really knew nothing about them. When she was about four months old, I decided to feed her an apple. I don't know where I got this idea, but I decided to teach her to paw for her apples. Within a week she was pawing for her apples. I always peeled them. People laughed as she got older, but she did not want them if they had peelings on them.

Over the years, Little Star was my friend. When I was feeling down, I would go outside and pet her, brush her, etc. She had the run of the yard. She was in her fenced area at night and when we were gone, but other than that she owned our yard! When I was in the yard, she was always close by. I remember a couple of years ago I got very sick. The doctors didn't know what was wrong for a few days. I would sit on the kitchen porch and cry and Little Star was always there for me. The doctors finally ran a sugar test and I have low blood sugar. That is why I was feeling so much in a daze. People wouldn't understand, but she would help keep me focused.

Well, I finally decided to breed her. A month before she was due to foal, I would hardly leave the house. Didn't sleep at all. My mother would get a little upset with me. She said what are you going to do when your kids have kids? But, I wanted so bad to be there if Little Star needed me. Well, my mother finally talked me into coming to her house one day. I rode up with my husband at 6:00 in the morning and went to my mom's. (I checked on Little Star before I left.)

At 7:30 a.m., my daughter called and said Mom, Little Star just had her baby. So I called my husband at work and he came, and we headed home. She had had a beautiful, perfect little baby boy. He looked just like her, only no star on his head. He is red with a white mane and tail. She let us touch him and check him without one single problem. She trusted us completely.

She had Star's Little Charmer (that is what we named him) on May 1st of this year. On May 14, Little Star and her colt were out in the yard with my husband and me. We looked over and Star was lying on the ground and we could tell something was really wrong. We both took off running. She was choking and foaming from the mouth—I can hardly talk about that part.

Well, of course it was after hours, but we called the vet and he said it would be faster to meet him at his office. So while my husband was hooking up the trailer (we have a small horse trailer now), I was putting Little Star's halter on. She was down and I was screaming and crying and praying. My husband kept telling me to get her up. I finally did; we both put her in the trailer, and as sick as she was, she threw an absolute fit until we got her baby in the trailer and then she calmed down. We finally made it to the vet's, a 40-minute drive. He put a tube in her nose and started pumping with buckets of water. My husband, myself and the vet worked on her for a very long time. She was finally unchoked, and not doing very good, but better.

By midnight the vet said he thought she would make it, but the next 24 hours were going to be the real test. The vet said she had choked on fresh grass clippings. We had just mowed our yard, but for years she had been in the yard after we mowed. I just didn't know this could happen to a horse.

We got about ten minutes from the vet's and Little Star fell over in the trailer. I couldn't get out. My husband pulled off the road, checked her, and got back in the truck and told me we lost her. I just couldn't believe it. Not my Little Star. I still can't believe it. I said let's call the vet just to make sure. So we called and took her back, and we had lost her. The vet asked if we wanted a necropsy to see what happened. I said no, so we buried her on our property. My husband used a bulldozer. I still haven't been able to visit her grave.

So, I was left with Little Charmer at only two weeks old. He would not have anything to do with the bottle. We even took him back to the vet and they kept him overnight and they could not get him to take the bottle, even after trying different types of nipples. So we decided on Foal-Lac Pellets. Little Charmer is now five months old and as healthy as can be. It was a tough road with him, but he is a fighter like his mother was. I had originally planned to sell him, but after what happened to Little Star, he has a permanent home with us.

My mother and sister stayed with me for two days, I was so upset. I still cry over her sometimes. Please don't get me wrong; my kids, my husband and my family are the most important things in my life. But, after them was Little Star.

I now own 19 miniature horses (I know, like everyone else I just wanted a pet). We even bought our first show filly this year. But I know in my heart no animal will ever take the place of Little Star.

Junie Moon Goes To School

By Joyce Salado
Highland Joy Farm
Grove City, Ohio

Junie Moon is going to school today, nothing unusual about that. And she is getting excited. Junie can tell it's a day to go to school, to a special school for children with disabilities. Every month Junie gets all cleaned up and ready to go. Junie walks right up the ramp into the van. Looking out the window, she knows where she is going, ears all perked up, a little nicker, and she will be there in just a few minutes. The children at the school are anxious for her to come again this month. The teachers put up a small portable pen for Junie to walk around in.

When the van arrives at the school, everyone is looking out the window. No time to study today, Junie is here! As soon as Junie is settled in her pen, a few children come out to greet her. They get to brush and pet her, and watch her nibble the grass and some hay. A student runs to get the bucket for water. Larry, a student who has read lots of horse books and is especially interested in horses, gets to help the younger students. Larry leads Junie up to the students so everyone gets their own turn to pet her and brush her. This is very special for Larry. He attends the special school because he is visually impaired; he is learning to speak, and you can understand his words now that he will talk to Junie. You see, in the past Larry would not talk to anyone. He was so shy and scared, and would run and hide, and scream for hours, and sit in class under the desk. That changed, slowly, when Junie started to come to the school. Now Larry is very outgoing and helpful with the other students.

Today Junie is startled by a lot of noise and crying just inside the doorway. Teachers gather around a new little girl, her first day at school. After her parents left, Gina was afraid. She had never been left in such a strange place with so many strangers, and she didn't know where she was. Gina was hit in the head with a baseball, and has brain damage. She had to learn everything all over again. Gina is 12, and really didn't want to be at school. It's time for Gina's class to go see Junie Moon. Gina says Ju moo. And doesn't want to go. It takes a couple of teachers and some students to calm Gina down so she can walk outside. Gina doesn't remember things like animals and friends, or toys— things every 12-year-old sees and plays with every day.

Larry is the first to talk to Gina, in language most of us can't understand, only making out a word or two, but you can tell how many times he's excited about saying Junie Moon. Larry takes Gina's hand to pet Junie, and she squeals and jerks back, scared. Junie walks closer to Gina, a little nuzzle on the hand, Junie says, its OK, Gina, I remember my first day at school too. A little more coaxing from Larry and Gina takes the brush, and lightly touches Junie's golden mane. A little giggle, and there is a big smile. It's not long until Gina gives Junie a big hug around the neck. The first day at school is now a great new beginning for Gina, thanks to the magic a little horse can work, and all the love and trust she has given to the special students at a special school.

Harriet Jennifer Justine O'Doul

By Harriett Rubins
Haligonian Farm
Canandaigua, New York
www.haligonianfarm.com

Harriet Jennifer Justine O'Doul
Was a wily old kid, was nobody's fool.
She knew about cities and alleys with junk,
She knew about drugs, saw some folks drunk.

But she was a scrapper and knew in her way,
She wasn't goin' down that road any day.
'Cause Harriet Jennifer Justine O'Doul
Was a wily old kid, was nobody's fool.

Harriet Jennifer Justine O'Doul
Set an example for kids in her school.
She worked hard to learn as much as she could
And helped friends 'n neighbors, hoped everyone would.

Like lugging bundles upstairs for Miz Fay,
Or scraping dog poop out of feet's way.
'Cause Harriett Jennifer Justine O'Doul
Was a wily old kid, was nobody's fool.

Now Harriet Jennifer Justine O'Doul
Had a wish in her heart, as strong as a mule,
She wished and she prayed in her bed every night
That everything wrong would someday be right.

The pavement with potholes, store awnings all torn,
Paint that was peeling, should be fixed by the morn.

And deep in her heart she longed for a park,
With flowers and fountains and lights in the dark.

Most of all, Harriett Jen Just O'Doul
Wanted a horse so bad she could drool.
She thought of them always from morning till night,
But felt in her life she'd not see such a sight.

She wished every night on the first star she saw
For a horse—just a small one would do, she was sure.
But maybe a park was a possible plan
So she wrote to the Mayor, got to talk with the Man.

Mayor Flynn liked the plan. "We need action!" he yelped,
And before she knew it—everyone helped.
They picked up the trash and hauled it away,
They filled in the potholes in less than a day.

Cracked windows were fitted with sparkling glass
Ripped awnings pulled down, fresh paint came to pass.
A little park bloomed in the lot cross the street
Mowed grass, many flowers—they all smelled so sweet.

But best of all, there in the middle of the park
Was a shed with a roof that was made out of bark.
And a paddock and gate that was sturdy and strong
It was oblong and grassy, wider than long.

And poised in the middle a sight to behold,
Two miniature horses, the color of gold.
They whinnied and pranced and bucked as they raced
The gathered crowd smiled at the girl they now faced.

Harriet Jennifer Justine O'Doul
Said Mayor Flynn loudly, "You're nobody's fool!
You had a dream and you made it ours too,
We finished it off with your dream come true."

On Frozen Pond

By Carrie Loffelmacher
Loffelrosa Farms
Graham, Washington
cloff@hotmail.com

I have a story to tell about a mini in my past, that I will never for-get. I have had big horses all of my life, and four years ago my horses and I acquired ten acres of our own in Washington State. I had the good fortune to move next door to a miniature horse farm. I had never been around the minis before, and they were so amazing to me. I had picked out a favorite and every time my horses got treats, so did he. And so my love affair began.

During the next year, I became friends with the neighbors and she taught me about the minis. I took a liking to a 34" stallion named Kappi, and started to play with him. The next thing I knew, I was watching driving videos and reading books, and Kappi was in cart and harness! To my neighbor's amazement, we were a match made in heaven. Soon after Kappi was in cart, he moved to my farm for what my husband thought was just temporary. Then on Christmas Day, my family and friends were over and the neighbor stopped by with the best Christmas gift ever: Kappi's registration papers signed over to me. I had always dreamed of a pony for Christmas; I just didn't think I would be 30 years old when my dream came true!

Later that same winter, we had some very cold weather; my pond froze over and so did my water tanks. I went to feed early one morn-ing and there was Kappi, frozen just like a popsicle. He had tried to get a drink of water and had fallen into the pond and somehow got-ten out. I grabbed him, the phone to call the vet, a blow dryer, and blankets. I brought him to the barn and tried to warm him up, but no such luck. The vet said to get some warm fluids down him. The barn was not warm enough and my blow dryer kept overheating, so I did what any normal horse person would do: I brought him inside the house, and turned up the heat. I put blankets in the dryer to cover him up, and brought him warm sugar water to drink. This did the trick; he started to look alive again. He stayed in the laundry room for most of the day, and was still in the house when my husband came home. I rushed outside to explain why the horse was in the house. He looked at me like I had finally lost my mind. Kappi went back outside a short time later, no worse for the wear, but I can say that he didn't go near the pond again.

Kappi.

'Twas The Night Before The Derby

(Or: How Derby Got His Name)

By Kent and Jennifer Hall
Triple H Minis
Benton, Kentucky
www.angelfire.com/ky2/triplehminis

A Letter To Derby's New Owner, Jill O'Roark of Whinny For Me Farm in Spotsylvania, Virginia:

Around midnight, Dakotah started having contractions and getting up and down as we watched on the observation camera. Once we arrived outside her stall, her water broke and the delivery began...all the signs were typical and normal, everything was textbook...out came a sac with the first obvious hoof and leg...it seemed to be extending longer...no nose following, no other legs...I went in to inspect and sure enough as I felt around we were going to have problems!

Jennifer immediately called the vet...it would be a 45-minute trip for him...we called some friends that have seen this before, they're ten minutes away and speeding to us now...at least five minutes have expired...time is the critical factor...Dakotah strains more with each contraction...we try to calm her...I try to gently return the protruding leg to perhaps allow another attempt...she squeezes my hand and forearm as I push slowly...I feel no nose or other leg...she wants me to leave her alone...I keep trying to no success...she tires quickly...ten minutes pass by, our friends arrive, he tries the same with no luck either...then he mentions needing some type of lubricant...vegetable oil is the best I could offer...after a $\frac{1}{4}$ bottle everything gets slippery...I make it in enough to feel its knee, she contracts and wants to break my arm off...in between her pushing and contracting I slowly advance...I make it to his chest...20 minutes have passed...the mare starts sighing and giving out...she starts relaxing more in between pushing...I desperately search for his nose as we know the baby is dead and we are trying to save the mare…I find his jaw, I try to determine where it's located and its position…25 minutes have passed…I follow his jaw to his nose, his chin is tucked downward to his chest…in between the laboring and pushing I reach in and pull the nose upward to its proper position…I can't feel the other leg anywhere!

Triple H Derby Day Miracle.

I go ahead and position the nose; in the next shove it's visible…30 minutes have passed…here he comes… as I help him out we discover the other leg tucked underneath his chin— thank goodness! The delivery comes quick now, like it's supposed to! The mare grunts and out he comes…blinking his eyes immediately…we realize *he's alive* and in perfect condition!

But all our attention turns to the mare…we do not want to lose her now! 40 minutes have passed…the foal is a colt and starts nickering and wanting up to see mama…he makes it up before she does. We hear the vet on approach…we feel much better now! He is surprised that we got him out alive…he inspects them and determines my birthing methods aren't the most aseptic so he cleans the mare and flushes her out and then doses an antibiotic…she finally gets to her feet and loves on her new miracle! Such a tear-jerking moment when mama and baby initiate the first bond and recognition, so precious! Especially after all of that!

The name came easy…we were looking forward to watching the Derby and this blessed event filled in the blanks…hence the name…Triple H Derby Day Miracle!

What an ordeal! But we established a great loving bond with him and it will be extremely difficult to say goodbye. You will be blessed with a special little horse that is here to fill everyone's life with joy and we are very happy to share this with you!

A Bag of Bones

By Judy Cates
Mini Appy Acres
Graham, Washington
miniappys@worldnet.att.net

I don't know whatever possessed me to buy the shaggy 30" pintaloosa mare and her foal. She was very thin and the colt was so thin, he was just a "bag of bones with a hide covering them." I just felt sorry for the both of them. They had been rescued from a bad situation and the person I bought them from had actually put some weight on the mare after deworming her and having her teeth floated.

The little fellow was in such bad shape, there was talk of having him put down. His hind legs kept locking up as he was trying to walk or run. He was so thin! There was nothing to him. He was about four months old when I got him, and he weighed maybe 35 pounds. I could pick him up without any trouble. After trimming his feet, and getting them both on supplements as well as Mare and Foal grain that is a 14% protein and good pasture, the weight started to come on both of them. The little fellow, whom we later named Brandy, was still having a lot of problems with his hind legs locking up. I was checking him over, going over his back and hips when I did find some warm spots that felt like mild inflammation from his joints slopping around. I came to the conclusion that because he had no meat on his bones, no flesh for ligaments or tendons, how could his joints stay in place. So, after he gained some weight, the sloppy joint problem started to improve, though he still had the hip/stifle problem. He still was not up on his pasterns as much he should be, as he still did not have a lot strength built up as yet.

A week after I had brought them home, my horse shoer for my Arab mare came to do her feet. I asked his opinion of the problems the little fellow was having; I had him check out his hips and back. He filed a little more off of his toes to set him up more to see if that would help. He then told me of a horse chiropractor that came to his place once a week to do the roper's horses.

A couple of days later he was to be there, so Brandy went to his first visit to the chiropractor. Brandy was in such bad shape, he could barely walk. After an assessment of Brandy and lots of adjustments to his back, hips, neck, and pasterns, he was not the same horse I had brought there. He was not only walking, he was trotting back to the trailer. It was amazing! Even the chiropractor was amazed at how well he was doing with just a few adjustments to get his body back into alignment.

Brandy.

Brandy had to have several more sessions over the next couple of months, at first weekly and then every couple of weeks. He was like a new horse. The person I had bought the mare and foal from could not believe Brandy was the same foal I had brought home. Other friends who had seen him said the same thing. They all thought I had performed a miracle. I just could not give up on the little guy.

Now as a yearling, Brandy has nice straight legs, and very nice conformation with a gorgeous little head. He is 31" tall and I doubt if he will grow more than ½" to 1". He is a buckskin pintaloosa. He hides his appaloosa markings under his fuzzy coat. He has teardrop-shaped markings over his hips when body clipped. And he has potential as a future show horse!

Pets Helping People

By Sue Brook
M&MS Farms
Williamston, Michigan
www.mmsfarms.com

It was a flyer on the post office wall that lured us into the pet therapy program at Ingham County Medical Care Facility (ICMCF). Violet Lentz, the volunteer coordinator, who started the pet therapy program some 20 years ago when she literally sneaked her mother's cat in the back door, was recruiting others to share small animals with the residents once a week.

The notice specified dogs and cats. Sure, we could do dogs and cats. And how about something different? How about a miniature horse?

We have a very special little mare who I knew would be perfect for the program. She's a retired champion show mare who was dropped from our breeding program after she nearly died herself giving birth, too early, to a dead filly. Soat's Lil Sugar & Spice, our little "Sugar," is a blue-eyed cremello and white pinto who already had lots of experience tending to people's special needs. She'd been part of Equine Hospitality Row at the Michigan State Fair; she'd worked with handicapped children; she'd participated in educational programs at day-care centers and churches; and she'd "done" children's birthday parties.

Although no horse had ever participated in the program, we got special permission to give it a try. So on the first Tuesday in November of 1997, Sugar jumped in the back of the van and made her debut as a therapy provider. Did she succeed? You bet!

Sugar adjusted almost immediately to the wheelchairs, gurneys, walkers, oxygen equipment and other paraphernalia the residents used. (In fact, did you know that walkers make great muzzle rests for little horses?) She enjoyed the attention. And as we were soon to find out, Sugar gave even more than she received.

When we went to pet therapy for the second time, Don, a stroke victim and former cowpoke who we were told could not speak, smiled and, with great effort, said Sugar's name. Another resident who refused traditional physical therapy reached out to touch Sugar. The little horse was a "miracle worker."

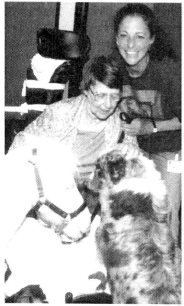

Angel, our half chocolate point Siamese cat, gives her warmth, softness and purring to almost any person who needs her. Rumor, our red merle Australian Shepherd, has an uncanny ability to know who needs her to jump up and give them kisses and who just needs to stroke her as she sits by their side. And then there are the pups the folks at ICMCF help us socialize and all the other dogs, cats and kittens who occasionally brighten the day for those who so look forward to "pets."

Why do we keep doing pet therapy when it takes special effort to arrange the flex time at work, change clothes,

Sugar, the pet therapist, with Sylvia Monsma, Rumor, and Sue.

hitch the trailer and make the trip in all kinds of weather?

When Sugar's ICMCF best friend Russell died in May of 1998, one week short of his 103rd birthday, we participated in his memorial service. At the luncheon, a card table was set up in the social hall, covered with pictures depicting this fine gentleman's entire lifetime. One of the pictures showed Sugar resting her head in Russell's lap as he sang to her and sweet talked her. Another showed Russell snuggling Angel. Sugar and Angel were that important to Russell. Russell was important to us. We do pet therapy to continue to honor that good man's memory.

We do pet therapy because it brings joy to Sylvia ("the cat lady"), who gave us a thank-you note for letting her help raise our kittens and a handcrafted angel to watch over us, and who now even looks forward to getting Rumor kisses. We do pet therapy for Maurie ("the treat lady"), who has her daughter buy "People Crackers" regularly just so she can be Rumor's and Sugar's favorite. We do pet therapy for Mary, who is blind and has no legs, but comes every week to "see" the animals and get kisses from Rumor. We do pet therapy because it pleases Violet, who can no longer remember enough to brag about her granddaughter's accomplishments, but who holds the cats and visits the other animals. We do pet therapy for Vera, who especially enjoys Sugar and Rumor, because she used to raise and train Standardbreds and Shelties. We do pet therapy for Ronnie, who just celebrated his 60th wedding anniversary but can no longer live at home with his beloved wife, and always greets us with a big hug and kiss and "Lollipups" for Sugar and Rumor. We do pet therapy for Dan, who sits up and smiles when Sugar "bops" him with her head or Rumor jumps up to kiss his face. We do pet therapy because it's a pleasant break for Leila, who desperately yearns for her brain seizures to end so she can go home to Lebanon. We do pet therapy for Maria, who spends most of the day by herself due to language difficulties but has no problem at all communicating in her native Spanish with the animals. We do pet therapy for Harry, who enjoys all the animals immeasurably. We do pet therapy for Joanie, who is blind, can't use her hands and is otherwise so disabled that she's wheeled in on a special bed, because she gets such pleasure from "holding" Angel and feeling her purr.

We do pet therapy for each of these people and for all the other ICMCF residents who enjoy pets so much on Tuesday afternoons.

We do pet therapy because it works—for ALL of us.

Postscript: Sugar was honored to be the very first miniature horse ever to win the Cosequin/Nutramax Exemplary Service Award for her humanitarian deeds. She formally accepted that award during the AMHA National Show in Fort Worth, Texas, in October 2001, with some 1,000 people in attendance. But her legacy award is what's really special: Cosequin will network with AMHA and AARP to promote the use of minis in retirement homes, long-term care facilities, and hospitals. So there's a good chance that what Sugar does weekly will be duplicated throughout the country, many times over, for years and years to come. Now that's special!

The Life of Annie

By Elaine Jones
Jones' Mini Whinnies
West Middlesex, Pennsylvania
http://jonesminiwhinnies.homestead.com/home.html

Annie was born on the 4th of August in 1992. Everything was fine, and it was an easy delivery. Our veterinarian was already scheduled to come out the next day, so we had him look over mom and baby. He said they looked great! We let them outside in a small pasture by themselves as we do all the new moms and babies.

On the eighth day, they came trotting in the barn for their evening meal, and Annie's mom dropped to the ground. She had suffered a heart attack and was gone in a matter of seconds. We sat beside her in shock and then started planning how to deal with an eight-day-old orphan. We called the vet and ordered some Foal-Lac, and until it came, we helped little Annie "steal" milk from other lactating mares.

Then we offered her a bottle, and she wanted no part of it, but she would drink her formula out of a bucket. Of course, we wore a lot of the formula because she was pretty sloppy, but at least she was eating. We took shifts day and night for nearly four months. Annie did great and seemed very happy, but we had a hard time convincing her that she was a horse and not a person. Eventually she learned to stay in the pasture and to be a horse.

In the spring, we clipped her and were so pleased to find such a beautiful mare under all that hair. We were anxious to show her so we planned a few shows. She did very well, and soon we were off to the Nationals. It was a long drive, and when we got there, we unloaded the horses and Annie didn't seem to look quite right. We had a vet look at her, but he couldn't figure out what was wrong. We continued to watch her through the night, and she seemed to be getting weaker and eating slower. We scratched our classes and headed home.

On the way home, she laid down in the trailer, so I said we were taking her to the Ohio State Veterinary Clinic. When we got there, the tests started. They suspected ulcers. Her protein level was dangerously low, so they gave her plasma. Then we had to decide to let them operate or not. We said "operate." Well, they did, but did not find any ulcers in the stomach where they would've been able to repair them, but they felt that the ulcers were in her intestines. They couldn't fix them, but the medication they had given her had already started to work and she was improving. Looking back, I wish we had said "no surgery." Now she had to recover from the surgery too.

Well, she did great and was a real fighter!

Annie went on to have six beautiful foals without any problems.

When her last foal was almost four months old, we found Annie lying upside down and tossing in her stall. We thought the ulcers were flaring up again. The ulcer medicine didn't give her any relief and we had more tests done. The results said it was not ulcers this time. Off to the hospital we went.

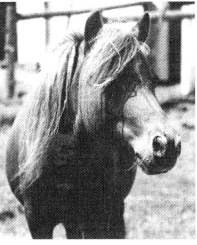

Annie.

After more tests, it was determined that she had twisted her intestine. There was no choice but to operate.

After opening her up, the doctors could see that this was going to happen sooner or later. Her secum was attached to her first incision site and a large section of bowel was twisted. She tried hard, but she couldn't make it through this surgery with all the complications.

So on July 2nd, 2001, we had to say goodbye to our Little Orphan Annie. We are very lucky to have had nine wonderful years with her and to have six of her offspring still with us. But nothing will ever fill the hole in our hearts when Annie left us.

God bless you, Annie. We will see you at the gates of Heaven.

Pets On Parade

By Terry Ann Heath
Heath Crest Miniature Horses
Middlefield, Connecticut
Heathcrest177@cs.com

It was announced on the radio that in January the Connecticut Humane Society was going to have a "Pets On Parade." People were invited to bring their pets to the Humane Society and compete for prizes in different categories: largest, smallest, most unusual, cuddliest, scariest, and furriest. When my son Eric heard about the last category, he said, "Mom, let's take a mini. Nothing is furrier than a mini in the winter." An understatement to anyone who owns a miniature horse.

We decided to take an 18-month-old filly, HH Blue Satin Bonnet. It was extremely hard not to clip or trim the filly, but when you are after the coveted "Furriest Award," you must leave on those long chin guard hairs and ear tufts. We groomed her until she was spotlessly clean and she even sported the luster of show coat spray, but oh, was she fuzzy!

When we arrived at the Humane Society, it was mobbed. Everyone was checking out—and petting—the competition. The filly was very popular, with a crowd of children keeping their hands warm by burying them in mini fur. There were at least 50 dogs present, representing all sizes from a toy poodle to a Great Dane. Over 25 cats were seen in all colors and ages. There were also over a dozen "miscellaneous" pets—rabbits, guinea pigs, hamsters, and one very fuzzy miniature horse.

The judges made their rounds. Every animal was on its best behavior (miraculous under the circumstances). Finally it was time to award the prizes. The largest: the Great Dane. The smallest: two baby guppies in a baby food jar. The most unusual: the iguana. The cuddliest: a monkey in a blue baby snow suit. The scariest: the Bull Mastiff. The furriest: the Miniature Horse!

The filly was unimpressed with her prize. She was more interested in a piece of the iguana's carrot.

When we returned home, we turned the filly back out into the pasture. She trotted over to the hay rack to be with her buddies. I must admit she did stand out—she was the cleanest furry horse in the pasture.

My Buddy

By Kathy Britton
Rolling Ridge Farm
Exeter, New Hampshire

We've been breeding and showing National-quality miniature horses for 15 years, and for many years before that I showed Arabian horses.

But this is about a special horse.

In April of 1995, one of my favorite mares, Twinky, was due to foal. She is a wonderful mother and had produced a top-selling show filly for us. Unfortunately, she had lost two foals due to foaling difficulties.

On this cold morning, after we had watched her all night, she foaled after being turned out. We rushed the baby (still attached to the placenta) and Twinky back into the barn. The little foal was shivering. We rubbed him down with warmed towels. After close inspection, we noticed he "wasn't right." He was a little odd-looking, and his legs were crooked. But he seemed healthy enough. He recovered quickly and began nursing on my fingers!

My husband suggested he might have to be put down. I informed him that I could never take this baby away from Twinky! If he did well, he might not turn out to be a great horse, but he could be my buddy.

Well, the name stuck. He stayed with Mama and she loved him as only a mother can who knows her baby is not "perfect." She waited for him to catch up with his little crooked legs before she would follow the herd, and kept watch over him for the next two years.

Buddy is six now, about 25" tall, and our farm wouldn't be the same without him.

Our beautiful show horses bring us National awards, ribbons and praise. Buddy gives us a personality and presence here on the farm. He can walk under fences and visit anywhere he wants. He talks to all the stallions, opens doors and checks all the stalls for leftover grain. Of course he's in charge of all the mares, even though he's a gelding!

Giving Buddy the chance to prove himself was worth every minute. He's very smart and seems to know he's handicapped. But as long as he's healthy and happy, he'll always be "my buddy."

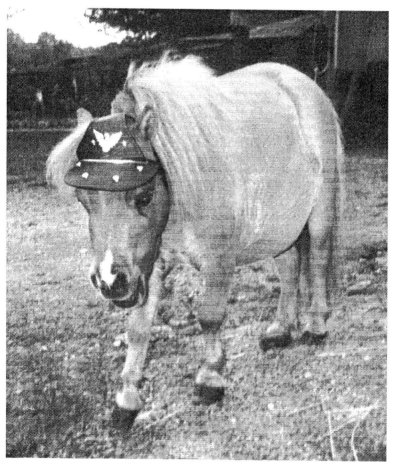

Buddy.

Born Too Soon

By Pat Elder
Rosa Roca Miniatures
Moore, Oklahoma
http://members.fortunecity.com/rosaroca

I found him first thing one morning, that mostly white pinto colt with the bay saddle on his back and the cap of color on his head. He was standing all alone, his little legs barely supporting him, his head hung so low that his muzzle almost touched the ground.

"Where did you come from, baby?" I asked, looking quickly around at my mares, none of whom showed any interest in the new arrival. My gaze settled on Bonnet, one of my medicine hat overos. Bonnet's hind legs were stained and her once plump belly was flat. Quickly, I gathered the little foal up in my arms and carried him to his mother.

The colt nuzzled half-heartedly at her side for a moment before Bonnet walked away. Lifting him in one arm and catching a handful of Bonnet's mane with my other hand, I took them into the barn. Once inside, the colt made another attempt at nursing, then folded his trembling legs and lay down. Mentally calculating how far away the mare's due date was, I called the vet.

An hour later, the colt was pronounced in adequate health. He had been given artificial colostrum to fill his little tummy and boost his immune system, along with a series of shots.

"Just watch him," the vet advised. "He doesn't seem that premature. Make sure he nurses, and call me if anything changes."

Once back in the house, I grabbed my breeding calendar. I blinked as I did the math. That couldn't be right! According to my calculations, only 295 days had passed since the mare was bred. I knew that foals with less than a 300-day gestation were not expected to survive. Even more worried now than before, I went out to check on my new little charge.

He was once again alone, lying much too still in the far corner of the stall while Bonnet munched on her hay. I went in and lifted his head, and was shocked to find the colt limp and nearly unresponsive. Hurriedly, another call was placed to the vet. Five minutes later, the colt was in my lap in the front seat of a friend's car, headed for the clinic. If he survived the trip, there would be time enough later to take his mother to join him.

"Come on, baby," I urged, rubbing and scratching at the brilliant white coat. "Don't give up now."

He revived, almost as if waking up from a sound sleep, and raised his head, taking in his new surroundings. Before long, he was standing in the alleyway of the vet clinic with a cluster of concerned people around him.

The prognosis wasn't good. As premature as he was, there was only a slight chance of survival. But I had to try. As the vets fell to work, hooking him up to an IV, I returned home to get Bonnet.

The rest of the day was spent there at the clinic. Whenever the little colt would make an attempt to stand, I would help him to his feet and guide him to his mother, steadying his head as he sipped at her milk. Every two hours or so one of the vet techs would arrive, listening to his heart and lungs and giving him food through a stomach tube and medicine through the IV. That evening, I reluctantly left him, knowing that someone would be there throughout the night to continue his care.

I called the vet clinic early the next morning, dreading what I would hear. But, surprising, the colt had made it through the night and seemed to be no worse. He was no better, though, either. As soon as the horses were fed, I headed back to the clinic.

The techs had taken quite a liking to the premature foal. One in particular said she had sat with him as much as she could during the night, holding him in her lap and talking to him. She said she had thought they were losing him at one time, when he had gone limp in her arms. But, a short time later, he had shown signs of life again and had even gotten to his feet by himself. He still wasn't nursing effectively, though.

I stayed with him throughout the morning, pleased to see that Bonnet had finally decided to pay attention to him. She would even nicker encouragement to him sometimes when he tried to nurse. A nearly constant stream of people stopped by the stall to see him. It seemed like he drew admirers like a magnet.

That afternoon turned hot. Despite the fans in the stall, the little colt seemed to wilt from the heat. The vet tech that was caring for him took him into the air-conditioned recovery room, taking him back to Bonnet periodically while she tried to get him to nurse. Meanwhile, his tube feeding and medicines continued around the clock. No one was still giving him very good odds.

Every morning, I called the vet clinic, half afraid there would be bad news. Each time, I was told that he'd made it through the night and that his condition hadn't changed. Then, I would go to the clinic and sit with him for awhile.

A week passed without much change. He would seldom get up on his own and couldn't stand for very long. Most of his nutrition was still via the stomach tube, but he was still trying to nurse, as long as someone stood beside him to steady his little head. On the morning of the eighth day, when I called to check on him, the vet came on the line.

"We're losing him, I'm afraid," Dr. Kent said sadly. "He's limp as a dishrag and won't even try to stand."

"He's done that before," I told him. "Several times, in fact. It's like he falls into a deep sleep and is hard to wake up. Keep stimulating him. Please don't give up."

The vet agreed, and by the time I made it to the clinic I was surprised to see the little foal standing unsupported at his mother's side, his head tucked under her belly. The vet tech flashed me a big grin.

"You were right," she said. "Dr. Kent and I kept rubbing him and finally he just 'woke up' and got right to his feet! I steered him toward his mother and he immediately started to nurse! If he's still doing well this afternoon, we're going to take them out onto the grass and let Bonnet graze for awhile."

"That I've got to see," I said with an answering grin. I returned to the clinic later that day. When I drove in, there stood Bonnet, happily munching on green grass, while all the techs and even the office personnel stood around watching the tiny little pinto colt as he got his first good look at the outside world.

"He looks great!" I exclaimed as I got out of the car. As if in response, the foal kicked up his heels and tried to buck. Everyone reached to help him as he fell to his knees, but he was up again before anyone could reach him. His next attempt was more successful. That out of his system, he set about exploring, running his little muzzle through the grass and up and down the tree trunks.

The next day brought even more changes. The stomach tube came out, as did the IV hookup. He still had his diet supplemented, but now he drank it from a large syringe, and he was still on medication. But, the vet said that would stop soon, too. It looked like the little guy had beaten the odds.

When he was ten days old, the still-unnamed colt finally got to go home. He would be delicate for some time yet, and a close eye would have to be kept on him. His premature lungs could easily get infected; his stressed immune system might leave him open for any number of nasty bugs. But he was nursing on his own and behaving like a normal, healthy foal. I started looking for a name for him.

"Million Dollar Baby" was my first thought, remembering with a wince the huge check I'd written before bringing him home. "Worth The Price" was my next choice, looking at his sparkling blue eyes and correct conformation as he trotted past me. Over the next few days, other names were laughed about and discarded such as "Born Too Soon" and "Almost Too Early." Finally, a name was selected, and the following poem was sent to the vet clinic along with a current photo:

We thought about our little one,
Long before he came.
Will he be a bay like Dad
With a silky long black mane?

Or will he look like Momma,
All patched in red and white?
Will he be born in daylight
Or in the middle of the night?

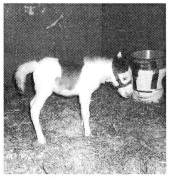

Willy in intensive care.

Will he grow up big and strong,
Or will he stay so small?
The one thing we never wondered
Was if he'd be with us at all.

He was born too early,
So weak he was barely alive.
But even then he was trying,
He wanted to survive.

We did the best we could for him,
And he touched each heart he met.
Everyone fell in love with him
But he wasn't healthy yet.

The medicines, the feedings,
They went on night and day.
But finally he came home to us,
On a very special day.

Just what will his future hold,
This one who came too soon?
Will he be a stallion
And make the ladies swoon?

Will he be a cart horse?
If so, he will go far.
Or will he be a show horse?
And Will He Be A Star?

Along with the poem was sent this short note: "Our sincerest thanks to each of you who spent so much time saving our precious little foal. He is three weeks old now, and doing well. We're sending you a current picture of him, and would like to introduce you to our future stallion and show horse, Rosa Roca's Willy Bea Star."

Well, our tiny, premature colt is now a robust two-year-old. He will begin driving training this winter, and will hit the shows next spring. He had a very shaky beginning, but one thing we are sure of: "Willy" will be a star!

Seed Money

By Virginia Cason
Diamond "C" Miniature Horses
Brownwood, Texas
rhcasonjr@verizon.net

A well-dressed couple with five children pulled into our driveway one sunny afternoon. They got out and explained that they wanted to see the horses we had for sale. After all seven looked over the herd very carefully, the youngest child, a little girl, was very, very interested in a gray filly we had for sale. The children were instructed to go to the car and did so, but the little girl kept looking back longingly at the horse.

The mother asked me if they could pay the horse out by the month as the little girl's birthday was three months away. We made the necessary arrangements for them to pay the horse out and they left. As they left, the child asked why they did not buy her this horse. The mother and father told her that they had to think about the other four children and their needs. She was not satisfied with that answer, so her mother told her that when she went to church, she must put "seed money" in the collection plate every Sunday, so it would grow into enough money for her to buy the horse and that she must also say her prayers daily.

The parents paid out the horse, and on the day of the child's birthday, her father borrowed a trailer and came to pick up Stormy. As is my custom if a horse is a gift, I do them all up in ribbons and bows on their mane and tail, and around their neck to make them look festive. The father was so pleased!

The father took the horse to the birthday party that was in progress. The child's delighted response was, "My prayers were answered and my seed money grew!"

The Night the Easter Bunny was Missing

By Lynn Heise
Rosebud Miniature Horses
Red Oak, Texas
http://www.geocities.com/rosebudminiatures/

It was a cool spring night, just at that twilight time prior to darkness, and I had just gone out to the barn to put the mares and foals in the paddock behind the barn for feeding time. I work a part-time job on Friday nights and the weekend, so Fridays are my busiest days as I work both jobs each Friday. As usual, I was hurrying to rush the mares through the barn where I had distributed their hay and grain. I thought I saw Easter Bunny run through the barn ahead of everyone else (as was his usual habit, as he is so small that he does not want to take the chance of being stepped on!), so I closed the back door of the barn and hurried on to work. All the way to work I kept questioning myself as to whether I had really seen him run through, or was it just my wishful thinking? It bothered me and I worried about it until I got off at 11:15 p.m.

Are you picturing a white bunny? Well, you're not too far off. Easter Bunny is my little dwarf, born the day before Easter in the wee hours of the morning in the middle of a big thunderstorm. It was also a Friday night when his mother decided to foal him, and I did not think she was due to foal for at least a couple of weeks yet, but since thunderstorms had been predicted, I shut her in a stall in the barn and went on to work.

Imagine my surprise when I entered the barn at 11:30 p.m. and heard what sounded like a goat bleating. I knew immediately upon entering that something was amiss, and rushed to the stall where I had settled in my pregnant mare only four hours earlier. I opened the door carefully and looked inside. I saw the tiniest little wet creature in the corner of the stall, halfway under the feed bin, staggering and bleating and shaking its little self. Oh, my goodness, it was tiny! I was shocked to see such a little creature in that stall. I rushed to it and picked it up in my arms, and it was very newly born, still wet from the mother's sac. I had no towels in the barn and it was chilly outside from the recent rain, so I brought some fresh straw into the stall and put it all around the little slippery thing, then ran to the house for some towels and warm water and a bottle of iodine. I was so aghast that the baby was so tiny that I brought with me a measuring tape, the kind you use in dressmaking.

I dried the little one with the towels and checked to see its gender; and quickly discovered he was a little colt. He was very fuzzy once dried thoroughly, and he had a very domey head, but his bite appeared to be very even and correct. He seemed to be in good proportion, but what worried me was that he was very knock-kneed in the front. He was very strong, and wanted to walk around on his own, and of course he was looking for his mother and her warm milk. He found her, but his little front legs were weak and they actually touched knee to knee, and he strained his short little neck for the nipples, barely able to reach them. His mother is 33" and he was very, very small. I held him up to her nipples and let him nurse for a few minutes at a time. This became tiresome quickly as he was heavy even for a little guy. Finally I returned to the house for a large syringe and a clean coffee mug, and milked out colostrum from the mother, then fed it to the foal with the syringe. I wanted him to have as much of this life-giving fluid as possible, so that he would have some immunity to germs and such.

Once I had gotten enough in his tiny belly to satisfy him for a short while, I took the measuring tape out of my pocket and measured him from the ground to the bottom of his mane. He was about 14½" tall as best I could tell, and I was amazed. This was the tiniest foal by far that had ever been born at my barn. Then I measured his leg, attempting to get a cannon bone measurement. It looked like about 4½". Could this be? Oh my goodness, I started getting a worrisome feeling that he might be a dwarf. I thought back about all the things I had read about dwarfs, and the pictures I had seen, and it was a definite strong possibility that he was just that. Now my worry was if he would be healthy enough to have a happy life, even if it ended up being a shorter life than the average horse. I decided I must call the vet as soon as it was light outside, and ask him to come by during the day to check foal and mother, give the foal a tetanus shot, and get his opinion on the dwarf possibility.

I stayed out in the barn the rest of the night, sitting in the stall with mother and foal, and for the most part held him across my lap and let him sleep there between feedings. I held him and loved him, then helped him reach mom's milk bag, then held him some more. He was a wonder in himself, so sweet and trusting and tiny. I fell in love with the little guy and knew he was going to need a lot of special attention if he was to survive in my tiny little herd of miniature horses.

Dawn came finally, so I went to the house to phone the vet. Poor man, he had been up half the night on emergency calls, so he was trying to get a little very badly-needed sleep, and I woke him up. But he was nice and thanked me for waking him, saying he had a lot to do and needed to get up anyway. He said he would call me back within the hour to get directions to the house again, as he had only been by a couple of times before and did not want to waste time searching when he could get some good directions. He was at the barn by about 9:30 a.m. and he was surprised to see such a tiny little creature too. He could not help but laugh at him, so tiny but so determined to follow his mother around the stall. He gave him his tetanus shot along with a vitamin shot and a mild antibiotic, as the baby had some diarrhea and I wanted to be sure he did not have any infection developing. The vet checked him over thoroughly and said he thought his legs would straighten up some in the front, and he would come back and see what he could do if they did not improve over the next week.

Then I asked the dreaded question, "Do you think he is a dwarf?", holding my breath and hoping he would say "No!", but he did not. He thought for just a moment, then said, "I wouldn't stake my reputation on it, but I am pretty sure he is." Then he added, "But he looks to be pretty healthy, and he has great willpower and zest for life, and a good bite, so if you can get him through the next week or two, he will probably have a pretty happy and normal life, just not as long as a normal horse."

Because he was born the day before Easter, and was tiny and light silvery cream-colored like an Easter Bunny, this became his name. I usually call him "EB" for short, and he knows I am talking to him or about him, make no mistake. He is and has always been full of himself, with a sparkle in his eye; and he cannot run through the barn without grabbing something in his mouth and running like mad to try and get it out the other side before you can catch him. He is little but he can really move fast when he is trying to get something over on you. His front legs straightened out a lot, but still have a slightly crooked appearance. He gets around like a champ, don't you worry.

But let me take you back to the night I thought he ran through the barn and out the back door...the night I worried about him until I got home from work. Of course I went straight to the barn to be sure he was there...and he was *not*...he was nowhere that I could see or hear, and I called and called, then listened for his little bleating voice, but heard nothing! The pasture is only 1.6 acres behind the house, and there is a guard light near the barn on the small side of the pasture, lighting the front of the barn pretty well. However, the rest of the pasture is pitch dark and you cannot see a thing without a powerful flashlight, not even a little almost-white Easter Bunny, not looking as hard as you can into the darkness and straining your eyes and ears, searching, searching. My heart was racing, and my mind was turning faster, faster, faster, running all kinds of terrible thoughts through my panic-stricken brain. Where was my baby? Had someone stolen him? After all, he was the cutest and tiniest thing that you could imagine. And he was so little that he could walk right under the bottom rail of the fence, and did sometimes, if the little neighbor boy came outside after school to talk to him. He would run right under that fence and go and chew on the little boy's pant leg and untie his shoelaces and follow him around the lawn, but never going more than ten feet away from the fence and his ever-watchful mother.

I continued to call him, then listen, call, then listen, hoping to hear some evidence that he was in the dark pasture looking for his mother or for me. I heard nothing. So I ran as quickly as I could to the house to get my big flashlight with the high beam on it. My next shocking and horrible thought was that he had gone under the fence, wandered into the neighbor boy's yard and fallen into their swimming pool...and you know what that would mean. I ran to the neighbor's yard and called him again. No sounds came from their yard. So I searched the fence around the pool to see if there was an open gate for him to get through, but there was not. That was a major relief for me. Then I went back into the pasture to try and look in the dark part of the pasture to see if he was out there, scared and alone. I looked in vain, as he was not to be found. My heart started racing faster as I tried to think of another answer to the mystery. My mind kept returning to the thought that someone picked him up and put him in their car and drove away. He was so little he would fit very easily on the floorboard of any passenger car.

The Easter Bunny (E.B.).

All of a sudden, I stopped in my tracks…I heard something! What was it? I listened again. There it was, a very weak little grunt. I ran around the side of the barn to the wire fence which surrounded the paddock behind the barn. Way at the far end of it, in the dark corner of the fence line, I saw him. He was nosed up to the fence, trying to reach his mother through the wire, and he could not reach her, the fence was in the way. He was so tired from trying to find her and get to her, that he could barely walk along the fence. And his normal happy little bleating was no more than a weak little grunt now and then. Oh, my heavens, I was so happy to see him! I ran and snatched him up and hugged him and hugged him, telling him all the while that I loved him and I was so glad he was OK! So glad that no one had taken him from me and carried him away. I carried him back to his mother around the barn and through the back door, and both of them were very excited to touch each other; it was a wonderful sight to see.

After I had time to calm down and sit down to think, Easter Bunny must have been asleep in the pasture when his mother came rushing to the barn, and he did not wake up until she was out of his sight and smell range. By then it was dark and he was alone and lost. He must have searched around for her and eventually followed her voice to the fence behind the barn. By the time I got home, he was just plain worn out from trying to reach his momma, so his little grunts were not loud enough for me to hear. He was six weeks old at that time, and still only 17" tall.

Life would never be the same around my place without EB. He is a wonder and a joy, and I am blessed to have him share my life…for how ever long I have him.

My Show Adventures

By Shade Tree Texas Brandy
(as told to Linda Wells)
Shade Tree Farms
Abilene, Texas

Hi, I'm Shade Tree Texas Brandy. If you attended any of the open Miniature Horse shows in Abilene, Texas, you have seen me. I'm the bay mare that loves to go into the ring and watch the people watching us. The other horses stand so still with their heads up and ears forward, while I look around and flick my ears to identify all the interesting noises I hear. Guess the other horses aren't people watchers, like me.

After the judge looks at us all standing in line, numbers are called and everyone begins to leave the ring. The first horse to leave receives a blue ribbon, the next one a red ribbon, etc. I'm usually the last one to leave. Don't know what that means for sure, but think people want to look at me…all by myself.

When we leave the arena, Linda (she looks after me) tells me what a good girl I am and sometimes even kisses my nose in public. I've heard people ask why she keeps going into the ring with me. She always tells them she loves that little bay mare and I give her an excuse to be where the action is. I think those people wish their horse had received my pastel ribbons, instead of those yucky blue or red ones. Sometime I'm so lucky I don't even receive a ribbon. Those times I must be "A No. 1," for Linda really makes a fuss over me. I like those times best of all.

Linda and Bobby (he looks after me too) have so much fun going to these shows. The other day I overheard them talking about taking me to the large sanctioned shows. They wanted to last year, but there was something about Bobby's health. In the last three years he has had three major surgeries. Don't know what surgery is, but guess that is when Linda feeds us all by herself.

Sure hope we get to attend those sanctioned shows this year. Bobby and Linda have gone to them before, but left us horses at home. When they returned, I overheard them talking about all the fun they had visiting with their show friends.

Bobby wants to take my palomino sister, Chug. Don't know why, she is always one of the first ones the judge makes leave the ring. Most of her ribbons are that yucky blue or red. Guess he shows her for the same reason Linda shows me, he loves his little --- now, can't say in public what he calls her in private. At home, he calls her the same name as the gray mare in Lonesome Dove. I hope my sister does better at the large show and wins those pretty pastel ribbons or better yet, she will be the last horse left in the arena.

Look for us at the show and be sure and clap when I'm in the ring all alone. All my people friends in Abilene do.

Oh, no! I just overheard Bobby say he wants to take an appaloosa yearling, Smoke and Ashes. He thinks she will do well in the multi-color classes. I don't want her to go with me and Chug, she has been so stuck up since her picture appeared in Appaloosa Network.

If Chug or Ashes happen to get the yucky blue or red ribbons, please don't let them know the pastels or no ribbon at all is best. I don't want their feelings hurt. Well, on second thought, go ahead and tell Ashes.

See you,
Brandy

Tribute to Havenbrooks Encores Blue Legacy

By Linda Rodriguez
Havenbrook Miniature Horse Farm
Burkesville, Kentucky
http://www.angelfire.com/biz4/havenbrook/

"Legs" was exactly what we had been waiting on, the kind of horse some breeders wait a lifetime to produce. When he was born there was no doubt he was a keeper! He had boldness and presence that caught your attention immediately, from his beautiful color, extreme "Dandy" action, and intelligent blue eyes, he commanded attention.

"Legs" was shown on a very limited basis. At his first show he won his class. His second show, "The July Classic" in New York, he received two seconds in a large class of more seasoned halter colts.

At the AMHA Eastern Regionals, he and his brother "Irish Cream" won Reserve Grand Produce of Dam.

We attended the AMHR Nationals, and the morning after he arrived home at the trainer's, he fell ill. He was treated by their Equine Practitioner throughout the weekend and suddenly crashed on Monday morning after having shown improvement.

Upon the vet's advice, they rushed him to Ohio State Veterinary Hospital. Sadly, he died en route.

Upon necropsy, no etiology was found that could explain the cause of death. All reports and tests upon completion were still unable to provide a cause, so we will never know for sure the reason he passed on. I guess God needed a very special friend for a little angel up there.

I will never forget you, Legs, you were my dream come true. I miss you, little buddy, you will remain forever in my heart.

The Legacy

All animal lovers believe in a magical place

Where their loyal companions go at the end of life's race

A land of green meadows, warm sunshine, and gentle rains

Where the animals frolic happily with no fear or pain

Legs.

They all know that someday they will be reunited again

With the humans who cherished them, according to life's plan

They must have needed a bright new friend today

So they called you home suddenly, no time for delay

Perhaps you were never meant to be here

Your high-spirited nature and boldness so clear

I named you "Legacy," for you invoked such dreams and big plans!

It is only now I realize your much higher purpose and truly understand

Go on my love, gallop swiftly away

I know you await our reunion someday

The wisdom within those bright eyes, so profound

I am certain you will show the timid and fearful the way to the sound

Of the animals playing upon the plains and the ridge

Which overlook the road that leads to Rainbow Bridge.

By Linda Rodriguez
Havenbrook Miniature Horse Farm
Burkesville, Kentucky
http://www.angelfire.com/biz4/havenbrook/
In memory of Havenbrooks Encores Blue Legacy